BACKSTAGE

Behind the Curtains with the Greatest Entertainers of the 20th Century - 2nd Edition

by Darryl Vidal and Martin Harrell—Copyright 2015-2016
Second Edition—Copyright © 2025 by Darryl Vidal

All rights reserved.

No part of this book may be reproduced, stored in a retrieval system, or transmitted in any form or by any means—electronic, mechanical, photocopying, recording, or otherwise—without prior written permission of the publisher, except in the case of brief quotations used in reviews or critical articles.

Illustration Disclaimer

The artwork contained in this book was created with AI-assisted illustration tools under the direction of the author and Crane Books illustrators. These drawings are intended solely for historical memoir and biographical purposes. Any likenesses to real individuals—many of whom are historically deceased public figures—are presented in the context of fair use for commentary and recollection.

Photograph Disclaimer

All photographs reproduced in this volume are the personal property of Marty Harrell and appear with his permission. They are presented exclusively for memoir, historical, and biographical purposes in support of the author's narrative. No commercial licensing of these photographs is granted beyond their inclusion in this publication.

Printed in the United States of America

ISBN: 978-1-969705-15-1

AUTHOR'S DEDICATION

To my parents, Eula and Clarence Harrell

My strongest proponents and my greatest fans. From my first instrument to my college scholarships, your unconditional support was the foundation of my musical success.

To my mother, for the loving edict to practice that I live by to this day. To my father, for always being there to listen.

This book is for you.

Martin Harrell

AUTHOR'S DEDICATION

This project is truly a work of passion wrapped in fun. I met Marty ten years ago at a golf tournament. As a fan of 50's and 60's pop culture, music, and witness to rock and roll's rise, I found Marty's stories unbelievable.

As he rattled off story after story about how he played with Frank Sinatra, Elvis and all these great personalities from the 60's and 70's I thought to myself, could he be telling the truth? His stories were only believable because he was the right age, and his friend/playing partner, Ralph Pressler, also a professional trombone player, vouched for him.

After every fantastic story about the Rat Pack and Sammy Davis, I would look over at Ralph, and he would just nod. By lunchtime I was convinced. As an author, I told Marty, "You have to write a book! These stories have never been told!"

He shrugged his shoulders and said, "That's what everybody tells me! But I can't, I'm not a writer!"

After the awards dinner, as we were all on our way to our separate cars and lives, likely never to see each other again, I couldn't walk away. I sought out Marty and said, "I am going to write your book."

We published BACKSTAGE. That was ten years ago.

It was a great thing. We both moved on with life. I've been writing and working. Marty has been playing golf, selling our book and he even recently got married.

I'm so proud of this book and I dedicate all the work to lovers of the genre. I hope this new second edition with additional stories and illustrations help tell some of the best gems of the 20th century. Enjoy!

Darryl Vidal

TABLE OF CONTENTS

Chapter One—The Early Days 1962—1965 6
- The Kidnapping of Frank Jr. 7
- The Tommy Dorsey Orchestra 23
- The Four Freshmen and Five Trombones 25
- The Les Elgart Band 30
- Race Relations 39
- Exchange Band 42
- The Camera Bug 44
- The Vegas Club, Dallas, Texas 47
- The South American Tour June 1965 51
- 1964 World Series 62
- 4th of July Mayhem 65
- Jack Jones meets Frank Jr. 72
- Dinner with the Sinatra's 74
- The Rat Pack—The Sands Hotel 76
- Frank's Gems 79
- Dino's Party Crash 82
- The Twin Palms 84

Chapter Two—Las Vegas Nights 1965—1968 87
- The Caesars Palace Band 88
- Pirate Kids 93
- The Exploding Bass Trombone 97
- Nelson Riddle 99
- Jack E Leonard 102
- Substituting for the Count Basie band 104
- The Fremont House Band 107
- The Comedians 109
- The Mills Brothers 110
- Unicycle Juggler 112

The Merv Griffin Show and Jack Sheldon	115
The Sword Juggler	118
Liberace	119
Sammy's Party with Connie	124
Satchmo's Gift Boxes	133
Burt and his Ponies	135
The International Hotel	136
Chapter Three—On the Road with the King 1969—1977	**139**
The Elvis Presley Orchestra	140
The Elvis Presley Orchestra	142
Marty and the Greatest Idea of all Time	145
On the Road	148
Not a Rock 'n Roll Band	151
The Opener	153
The Sahara Tahoe House July 1971	155
Pedal E & the Lowest Notes Ever Recorded	160
The Cincinnati Hilton(s) November 1971	164
Live from Hawaii—1973	167
Opening Night Baton Rouge, LA	170
Black Angel	174
Memphis Stop 1974	175
Girls, Girls, Girls…	179
Elvis' Easter Bunny	182
Snowstorm in Pittsburg	186
Chapter 4 - End of an Era	**189**
The Crab Car	190
Unchained Melody	196
Tour 6—August 1977	198
Video References and Endnotes	**204**

Chapter One—The Early Days 1962—1965

The Kidnapping of Frank Jr.

December 8, 1963

Wind and snow were more typical of Midwest weather where Marty had grown up. Not so much on the West Coast, although South Lake Tahoe was at a very high elevation and wind, cold, and severe snowstorms could roll in and out of the Northern California High Sierras spectacularly.

Southern Indiana lies in the transition between the Great Plains and the Appalachians where severe weather from tornados to torrential rain could fall to make for a variety of weather patterns. Marty was very familiar with the "flatlands" throughout his youth, but these were real mountains, unlike the 4-5,000-foot peaks he had seen before.

Having traveled from the much warmer climates of Phoenix and Los Angeles two nights before, Marty and the rest of the Tommy Dorsey Orchestra were gearing up for a six-day circuit of Tahoe and Reno. It would be the first time back in very cold weather and snow since he left his home in Indiana.

It was a good thing they were well prepared with heavy jackets, gloves and snow boots. The weather was sure to make for an interesting few days that would change their lives forever.

In the winter of 1963, there were three casinos in Tahoe: Harvey's, a casino with a hotel, Harrah's, a casino with a small motel, and a casino named Barney's. They were the center of nightlife of the South Shore and became hugely popular with the Las Vegas and Hollywood types for some winter wonderland fun. Only an hour from Reno, and two hours from

Sacramento, the South Shore Room at Harrah's Tahoe was the most recently built and included a 750-seat showroom which brought the best of live entertainment to Stateline. The casino had a modest motel across the parking lot. Entertainers like comedian Red Skelton, singer Barbra Streisand, and pianist Liberace made for spectacular nightlife as an addition to the snowy winter vacation town. The actress who made the biggest run this year was Judy Garland.

That night in December '63, the South Shore Room of Harrah's Tahoe Casino lounge was brightly lit, uproariously loud, and smelled of tobacco smoke, stale perfume, cheap whiskey, and maybe a hint of ammonia, bile and stench. Late for a scheduled dinner with the band's singer and trumpet player, Marty made his way from the Harrah's Casino lounge, where he had been sharing a drink and stories with Ernie McDaniels, the bass player for the Mary K Trio. Marty and Ernie had known each other for many years, playing together but hadn't seen each other for a couple of years.

Marty stepped outside into the bluster of sideways snow-flurries and the scream of the High Sierra winds slashing through the Lake Tahoe basin. Bundled up in snow boots and a winter jacket, he pulled up his collar to prepare for the bitter cold hike through climbing snow drifts to the motel across the frozen parking lot.

He made his way out of the lounge into the bitter cold. The wind blew fiercely, and snow fell in chunks as it fell off the giant redwoods lining the highway and parking areas. It had been snowing for days and now it was coming down hard as the moon rose to light up the snowy drifts. The smell of wood burning in stoves and diesel from the snowplows, mixed with the chill wind and stinging snowflakes to turn the California/Nevada vacation town into an alien landscape.

The band would be playing in the lounge tonight at 10pm and again at 2am, and Marty was supposed to finish dinner with Frank Jr. and John Foss by 9:30pm so they could prepare for the shows and what would have been the start of another great tour with the Tommy Dorsey Orchestra.

The motel was a two-story bungalow style with exterior stairways, so the walk upstairs was totally unprotected from the elements and a slip and fall on these stairs could be bad for your health and head. A chill-to-the-bone ran up his spine as Marty could see someone coming toward him, but the familiar form was unclear from the blizzard conditions and the heavy clothing. Suddenly, from across the walkway, John Foss, trumpet player with the Tommy Dorsey band, stopped Marty in mid-step and short of breath.

"They've taken Frank!" He shouted above the wind as he shielded his face from the blowing snow.

"What?"

"They've kidnapped Junior!"

"Who?" Marty had no idea what the excitable trumpet player was talking about or if this was some kind of practical joke. "What the hell are you talking about?"

John didn't know who or what. He and Frank Jr. were waiting for Marty, having a room service dinner, when there was a knock on the door.

"Special Delivery!" was declared following the knock. John answered the door half-expecting Marty or some other band member. As he cracked the door open, two men dressed in black jackets and ski masks burst through the door knocking him to the floor. One of the two hoodlums pointed a small revolver at them and calmly told the musicians to lay down on the floor, face-down. They used duct tape to wrap their wrists and ankles, and taped their mouths shut.

"Just stay put for 10 minutes or we'll kill Frank," were the instructions John detailed to Marty, and then again later to the police. The kidnappers obviously knew who they were dealing with. Somehow they had identified Frank's room #417 down an interior hallway.

Their trial testimony would later reveal that Barry Keenan, the ringleader, had been following Sinatra Jr.'s tour and watching his performances with the Tommy Dorsey Orchestra for the last several weeks. He had visited Harrah's ahead of time to case the property, and get familiar with the backstage and hotel layout. They even asked the staff where the singer's room was and watched him enter and exit the room several times to lay the groundwork for the abduction.

Back then, there were very minimal security and safety procedures to protect guests. Entertainers and their entourage often moved freely between the stage area and hotel rooms without much staff interference.

The two hoisted the bound and gagged son of the greatest entertainer of the time, and carried him away, assumedly out to a car or truck. John waited a few minutes and then wrestled and wriggled his way out of the duct tape that had bound him.

By the time he found Marty heading to the room, John had already alerted Tino Barzie, the band manager who was in the room next door. Tino had made the first call to the police and got things rolling. That's when he ran outside to find Marty on his way to meet them for dinner. The trumpet player was still in shock.

With nothing to do but wait for the police to arrive, they thought they should be able to follow or track the threesome's footprints in the snow. The lighting in the parking area was dim, but the moon was out, giving some degree of visibility, but nothing could be more futile. Within minutes, the new falling snow covered any clues to the kidnappers' escape with Frank Jr. in tow. Obviously the two shows scheduled for 10pm and 2am were canceled until further notice.

Police responded and set up a dragnet of roadblocks on both the California and Nevada-bound directions on Highway 50 within minutes of the kidnapping. The roadblocks and inclement weather clogged the streets of Lake Tahoe South Shore into the night.

As many as 35 Lake Tahoe police officers were engaged to search nearby summer homes and backroad areas as the night wore on. Police believed that since the roadblocks were up so quickly, the kidnappers must still be in the South Lake Tahoe area, hiding out in one of the many summer vacation homes or possibly in the deeply forested areas.

The Douglas County Sheriff stated, ""I think they are still up there in the area. We had all the highways blocked within 10 minutes of the kidnapping." Douglas County Sheriff's Deputies armed with sawed-off shotguns and pistols searched through boarded up cabins and summer vacation homes in the Zephyr-Cove Glenbrook and Spooner Summit areas through the night with no leads.

The news hit the nation just like the Sierra snowstorm. The morning headlines made the biggest splash since the Lindbergh kidnapping. The son of the Golden Boy, "Ole' Blue Eyes," Frank Sinatra Jr. had been kidnapped.

As kidnapping is a federal offense, the FBI was immediately brought in to take command of the situation. Sinatra may have been the most "connected" personality in the nation having the (former) President of the United States and his US Attorney General brother as close personal friends. Direct phone calls were made from Washington to the Palm Springs residence of Frank Sinatra.

The closest federal office was near Reno, Nevada. Typically, a one-hour drive on the forested highway up to Lake Tahoe but on this particular evening no one could get into Tahoe either from the California side or the Nevada side. By morning, the first of the FBI team were making their way to investigate the latest "crime of the century."

Martin "Marty" Harrell had auditioned for the Tommy Dorsey Orchestra in 1962 while touring the Midwest with the Les Elgart Band. A very popular "dance" band of the big band era where Marty was the bass trombone player. The Tommy Dorsey Orchestra was led by famed conductor Sam Donahue who had the idea of bringing the band on a 40's and 50's "nostalgia" tour of the Western states, including Phoenix, Los Angeles, Las Vegas, San Francisco, Reno and Lake Tahoe.

Marty was one of the youngest in the band at a tender 19 years of age and this is where he would first meet Frank Sinatra Jr., who was the singer of the Tommy Dorsey band and just starting his career as front man—just like his father. Being the same age, they became roommates, toured together and would become lifelong friends.

Frank Jr. was an incredibly friendly and likable young man. Many would think that as the son of the legendary singer, he might have a bit of an entitled attitude, but Frank was just as approachable and sincere as anyone else. Their friendship would emerge from their road trips together and ultimately would last both their lifetimes.

Marty would recall a lecture from Nancy Sinatra (Barbato—Frank Jrs. Mother) that was a great lesson in humility for both Frank and Marty. The band was on its way to Japan and then to the Philippines on an Asian tour. It was the first time overseas for Marty and he was heeling up to Nancy Sinatra in the absence of his own mother—an inexperienced overseas traveler that he was. As they made their way through the terminal at LAX, the son and wife of the legendary Sinatra gathered a trail of photographers, reporters and other onlookers. Having the legend's son as frontman crooner, brought with it great publicity as well as the paparazzi.

The assortment of media types and curious fans raced to get in front of the band and between the band members in order to get a shot of Frank and Nancy, even though they were among the larger group of musicians and managers of the Tommy Dorsey Orchestra. A reporter appeared out of nowhere and stuck a microphone in front of Frank's face and the mob began to stumble. A human pile-up ensued as they approached the gate.

Because of the ruckus, Frank Jr. asked the group of paparazzi and spectators loudly, "Please! Make way, so we can get on our plane."

The group cleared away, reacting to the loud admonishment from the young Sinatra. After they got on the jetway and the non-travelers were out of sight, Nancy called Frank to the side and said, "You aren't your father. If you're going to earn the respect of these people, you're going to need to treat them like professionals." It was an important lesson for the impressionable young men.

Marty recalls the long trip to the first stop, Hawaii, then on to Japan and finally the Philippines. The three sat together in the same stuffed row, Marty on the aisle, Frank Jr. at the window and Nancy squashed between them for 12 turbulent and droning hours.

Marty had thrown together his traveling outfit. He really didn't have a lot of clothes. All he really had was his band outfit and some casual slacks, a couple of old button-down shirts, and a dusty Navy-blue blazer that was missing a button. Nancy took inventory of the rumpled skinny kid sitting between them and asked Marty to take off the jacket and hand it over. Out of nowhere, she produced a travel sewing kit, removed a needle and thread, and affixed a new button on the blazer.

Back in Tahoe the band members were devastated. Although they all knew Frank Jr., would be a prime target for a kidnapping, with the great wealth and high profile of his father, they still couldn't believe it had actually taken place. And there was so much to be concerned about.

With the tour on hold the band members gathered in the hotel and club and worried, smoke cigarettes, cry and hope for the best. News was sketchy and repeated over and over. The most reliable updates came from the local police.

Frank Jr. wasn't only their star front man but was beloved by them all. They couldn't help wishing and hoping for his safe return. So as news of Frank Sr.'s involvement was revealed, a glimmer of hope began to emerge.

Marty and John Foss were initially detained, questioned, fingerprinted and kept under police protection as authorities still had no idea who was responsible and what was their intent. Because they were touring together by bus, they had little choice but to stay at the motel and aid in the investigation and help keep the other band members' hopes and prayers up—besides, they were also snowed in.

Frank Sr., very upset, flew his private plane from Palm Springs into Reno, Nevada and called in to the local police and offered $1 million dollars cash to the kidnappers. He tried to get to the Lake Tahoe area but because of the winter storm, he was forced to stay in Reno. The famed singer and his crew set up headquarters in the Mapes hotel in Reno, the most prominent luxury hotel in Reno at the time.

Sinatra had stayed there often when performing in northern Nevada. It became the Emergency Operations Center for the duration of the case. There, Frank Sr. and his entourage, waited for some word or communication from the kidnappers.

As many as one-hundred California and Nevada Sheriff's Deputies and 26 FBI agents converged on South Lake Tahoe and joined the snow-bound manhunt.

The next day the FBI arrived and took over the investigation. US Attorney General Robert Kennedy, still reeling from the assassination of his brother President John F. Kennedy less than a month previous, promised Frank Sr. the full resources of the FBI and Justice Department in the hunt.

Back in Tahoe, Marty and John were taken by the FBI to the sealed hotel room. He was told to put on a trench coat and keep his hands in the pockets while they questioned him inside the room, presumably to minimize fingerprints and disturbance or contamination of evidence.

The room service cart, dinner (chicken), glasses of wine and other items littered the room. Marty was able to identify some items out of place and Frank's belongings, but it didn't look like there was much of a struggle and no additional evidence or clues were found—and nothing pointing to the party responsible.

Then they were taken into the Casino and asked to identify anyone who might have been in close contact with Frank Jr. before the kidnapping. One or two ladies Marty knew were identified but these interviews led nowhere. The kidnappers had been surveying their prey for several weeks and were careful to keep their activities discrete.

The crime made national headlines as the kidnapping of the son of the world's most famous singer hit the morning papers and then the evening news. One picture of Marty being escorted into a police car made the

Associated Press (AP) and was seen by his mother in Indiana, who didn't know what to believe. A call to his home later set Mrs. Harrell's mind at ease. At least her son was safe and not part of this ill-conceived crime of the century.

As the second day wore on, the roadblocks and snowstorm and the entire city of Lake Tahoe remained on lock-down but there were no traces of Frank Jr. or his kidnappers. Some speculated they had escaped into the mountains.

Short on staff because of the storm, Marty was engaged by the local police to stay in the room and was assigned the duty of answering the phone. People from all over called the hotel to ask about Frank Jr. and were connected to the room. Marty spoke with many friends of Frank Sr., who were concerned and offered to help. Ava Gardner was one. Alan Ladd offered to have horses flown up to help track the kidnappers in the snow. Call after call was answered with not much information to offer.

By the following morning, December 10th, the second day following the kidnapping, Frank Sr. was receiving ransom calls at his command center at the Mapes hotel from somewhere in Southern California. Clearly the kidnappers had escaped clean on the first night.

It was believed that they covered Frank Jr. with blankets in the rear of a white Chevy Impala and escaped using the ruse through the roadblock on Highway 50 South into California. The dragnet was shut down and now the FBI focused on advising Frank Sr. on gathering the money, $240,000 was the ransom requested—and noting all the serial numbers so that the money could be tracked later. It would be ironically noted that Frank Sr. originally offered $1million ransom, but the kidnappers obviously didn't know and asked for the much lower amount.

After several phone calls to various phone booths in the Sparks, Nevada area, the kidnappers finally gave Frank Sr., specific instructions for the money drop at a location near Los Angeles. Frank Sr. would pilot his own aircraft to a designated airport near Los Angeles and then personally drop the briefcase of small bills containing $240,000.

Once picked up, Frank Jr. was released on a freeway off-ramp near Mulholland, a couple of miles from his mother's Bel Air home. The FBI would later find out that the kidnapper holding Frank Jr. panicked and released him even before he knew the pickup was made.

Marty and the whole Tahoe contingent knew nothing about the money exchange and the release of Frank Jr. until after the transaction was complete. They had at least an additional day of worry and prayers before they got the news a full 24-hours after the rest of the country, while they were trapped in the Sierra snowstorm.

Each band member took a collective deep breath and blew their nose one last time as they got the good news. Frank Jr. had been returned home in Southern California, and he was safe and in good health. The Tommy Dorsey Orchestra, and the rest of the nation drew a sigh of relief to the not-so-terrible ending of the caper. Details of the money transfer would come out later, along with the capture of the three kidnappers.

Unfortunately, speculation turned to rumor, then to conspiracy. First, it was the defendant's positing that they were being framed by Frank Sinatra

Sr. as a publicity stunt to boost his son's career. Then, there was speculation in the Hollywood rags that would place Frank Sr. himself as the key conspirator. None of these explanations made sense as the incident cast a pall over the budding career of Frank Jr.

Was the kidnapping a stunt to boost the younger Sinatra's debut? Marty will tell you unequivocally—NO WAY. Though this specter would cloud Frank Jr's. career for many years.

The incident would also mar Frank Sr's peace-of-mind for many years. He was deeply disturbed to be alleged by some to be behind the plan to boost his son's career. He even carried rolls of dimes with him for several years—in case he needed to make emergency calls from a pay phone—part of the ordeal he suffered in the ransom drop.

* * *

On reflection, Marty recalled during the Phoenix run of the tour, there was a strange occurrence that might have been tied to the kidnapping. Both Marty and Frank Jr. loved the outdoors and the early winter briskness of the cool, dry desert air. A ranch near the hotel offered horseback riding.

Both Marty and Frank were experienced horseback riders and both loved to take the animals for a trot through the brush and cactus before morning rehearsal. The smell of dust and creosote was a welcome reminder of the desert that was mysteriously exhilarating. Combined with the relaxed pace of the horses, these outings were an important distraction from the musicians' nightly performances and daily bus touring.

Frank drove a black Pontiac convertible which was left in the hotel parking lot. On this day, after returning from riding, they found Frank Junior's convertible top slashed by a knife. No other clues were left of the vandals or their intent, but it may have been a foreshadowing of the night in Tahoe. Later, Marty and Frank speculated that the kidnappers tried to grab Frank Jr. that day but were thwarted because of their time out on the range.

The trauma of the kidnapping ordeal was something that Marty could empathize with and out of sensitivity and consideration, never spoke about, even 50 years later.

Cops stop a car at barricade near Stateline, Nev., shortly before all roadblocks were suddenly cleared away.

RENO EVENING GAZETTE

Storm Backs Up Roadblocks
KIDNAPED SINATRA HUNTED

Singer Abducted From Lake Motel

Sinatra Kidnap Account

Consequences
Americans Still Held In Bolivia

SINATRA FRIEND AND MANAGER TELL OF KIDNAP

SINGER TAKEN AT GUNPOINT

The Tommy Dorsey Orchestra

Marty started playing trombone in elementary school. As part of the 5th grade arts curriculum, the school would assemble an orchestra. Any student interested in learning was encouraged to pick an instrument and become part of the orchestra—no experience required. Looking back, Marty believed that this basic offering and encouragement at this early age was a major factor in his discovering the talent that would take him on the journey of a lifetime.

As the orchestra was being selected, each student was asked to pick an instrument. They had a choice between strings, horns and percussion. The violins looked complicated to Marty, but ultimately the reason he picked the trombone was because they had to form lines to get their instruments. Marty hated lines so he went to the shortest line, it was for the trombone.

Marty would learn that it is important for beginning students to have quality education in music. It started with the fundamentals and went from good rhythm, timing and just plain practice, practice, practice.

Thinking back to his high school days Marty never dreamed he would be playing behind the greatest entertainers of their time, but strong fundamentals and a little creativity could go a long way when it came to playing in the orchestra.

At the University of Indiana, Marty studied under some of the greatest horn players of his time. Starting with Dr. Tom Beversdorf and Buddy Baker, both renowned swing and big band players, and his most influential teacher, Bill Bell. A talented tuba player who played with the New York

Philharmonic Orchestra. It was under his tutelage that Marty refined his bass trombone style.

One day, the tuba player renowned for his recording of "Tubby the Tuba," advised Marty, "Sit down son. If there's one thing in life I can tell you, you have to set goals. Strive to achieve them and then set more. It is a constant process of working and setting greater goals."

At the time, Marty was studying under a performance scholarship and working at a local golf course. It was there, while riding the tractor, mowing the fairways that Marty thought about his goals based on the inspiration of Bill Bell.

"I'm going to play bass trombone for Frank Sinatra" he told himself. That was his goal. And Bill Bell was not one to tell him that he was crazy. What, with the career advice he had just handed out. Of course, Bill Bell had never played with Frank! Within two years of that promise, Marty would first play for the legend's son, Frank Jr. and then within the next two years, he performed bass trombone in the orchestra behind Ole' Blue Eyes himself.

Bill Bell's advice proved to be as much prophecy as strategy.

The Four Freshmen and Five Trombones

The Summer of '61 was the end of Marty's freshman year at the University of Indiana. One of the biggest hold-over bands in the late 50's had seen their fame start to wane as Elvis and the Rock and Roll phenomenon started to attract the attention of the younger set.

The Four Freshmen were a male vocal quartet that blended the jazz-arrangements with big band group vocals. The Freshmen were heavy on melodic harmonies and complex vocal gymnastics that became a named influence of later bands such as the Beach Boys and the Mamas and the Papas. Brian Wilson attributes some of the Beach Boys harmonic approach directly to his study of their recordings.

Several years earlier the Four Freshmen and their leader, founding member Bob Flanigan released their breakout album "Four Freshmen and Five Trombones." This album was called the new standard for modern jazz vocals and actually reached number six in the billboard Top 10.

At the time Marty was finishing high school, this album was at its peak of popularity, with the Freshmen touring college campuses in an effort to bring the big band harmonies to the rock and roll crazed kids. This inspired Marty to assemble his own jazz trombone band in hopes of playing with the Four Freshmen one day should they make the circuit through his stomping ground.

His goals and strategy once again paid off. Later that Summer, Marty had seen a promotional advertisement of the Four Freshmen coming to Indiana University in the Fall. Marty decided that his trombone quintet was every bit as good as the Five Trombones from their 1955 album and that his group should back up the Freshmen for the IU event.

It took a bit of research, but Marty was able to discover the agency handling the Freshmen through the event manager. From there a couple more phone calls, messages left, and more follow-up calls, and Marty found himself with the phone number of none other than Bob Flanigan. Bob was more than gracious as he listened to Marty's pitch. Little did Marty know that this friendship would last both their lifetimes.

Marty proclaimed, "Look, we've got five trombones. I play bass trombone. We're all college level performance musicians here at IU and we know the whole album." The phone was quiet for several seconds.

It didn't take long for Bob to see that this was a great idea, especially since they were doing a college tour, what better promotion than to have a college horn section to fill out the performance. This was the exact cohort they were targeting.

"Well, since it's only the Four Freshmen on this tour, it would be a shame not to take you up on your offer. If you're all as good as you say!" Marty stated, "Our excitement was off the charts. We'd listen to the tracks from the phonograph and play it back, over and over… To where we could even do ad libs in time."

It would be the biggest crowd the five teens had ever played to. At the time, the Four Freshmen were as big as Elvis and the Beatles in the 60's. The boys got their professional chops that night. No more collegiate-level stuff, Marty and his boys were going to hit the big time!

The performance went so well that they were invited to play the following scheduled performance at Purdue University 200 miles away from Marty's hometown of Evansville. And they were going to get paid! They just needed to be there for a quick rehearsal before showtime the next day.

Marty had to borrow his dad's white '59 Plymouth Valiant to make the trip. The old type with the push button transmission on the dash. It would be the first time Marty would drive that far without his mom or dad in the car with him. The five boys carefully packed their trombones into the trunk and loaded their bodies into the car.

It was a little tight for all five, but they didn't need any luggage because they were going to just turn around, grab some food, and make the 4-hour drive home after the gig. It would prove to be another great gig with the biggest band touring the Midwest at the time.

After another successful night with the Freshmen, and promises to do it again, the boys loaded back into the Valiant, went through the drive-thru for some burgers and shakes and headed for home.

It was halfway or so into the trip home. The boys had eaten their burgers and were starting to nod off. Marty's eyes were getting a little droopy but nothing that the large chocolate malt couldn't correct. The two-lane country roads through central Indiana were flat and straight but dark.

Streetlights only came and left with the major stop lights and infrequent gas stations on the late-night journey. The lonely trip was typified by long stretches of darkness, where the only thing the driver could see were the lines on the road and the endless row of fences bordering the vast farmlands of the Great Plains. The fence posts zipped by like flashing toothpicks racing by and the low rumble of the Valiant purring down the asphalt could lull the unwary driver into a trance.

Every now and then Marty would be blinded by the high-beams of an oncoming vehicle which would focus his attention like a laser-beam for several seconds and serve to keep the tired teen musician focused on this critical errand of getting every boy home safely.

Every few miles Marty would guide the Plymouth around a slow-moving semi-truck or the occasional combine moving between farms. Marty opened the windows as he let the warm summer night air breeze through the car as the boys all seemed to fall into a deep burger-induced slumber.

Just as suddenly, a low white flash cut across the high beams and Marty reflexively yanked the steering wheel right. The large dog stopped and turned 180 degrees around and completely avoided getting run over by the Valiant blazing down the road at 80 miles per hour.

The car ran off the road and onto the dry, dusty shoulder that wasn't too bumpy but made for an uncomfortable awakening for the four sleeping teens. The car bounced up and down as Marty wrestled the car back into control and over a fence post and side-swiped the next post before popping back onto the roadside.

Marty stopped the car and took inventory of his weary cargo, who were too drowsy to be scared out of their wits. Everyone was okay, but it was too dark to get out and inspect the damage. Cars seemed to be buzzing past like lighted missiles in the dark and it wouldn't be safe to stay there stopped on the side of the road so Marty decided that they would just limp the car back home as planned.

Home safely the boys were dropped off individually that night and Marty parked the mighty Valiant that had guided them home safely in the driveway. Too tired to break out a flashlight, Marty headed off to bed.

"What the hell did you do to my car!" Were the first words Marty heard as he woke up the next morning. Shaking off the cobwebs, Marty could see the upset face of his father and reminded himself of the previous night's adventure.

He recalled the burgers and shakes, the sleeping cargo, and of course the rough interlude into the fence posts. The damage to the bumper was not as visually disturbing as the sweeping dent and scratches along the side of the formerly pearl-white stallion, but after an explanation, and understanding that no one was hurt, Marty's dad could not be prouder of this son.

The Les Elgart Band

After a year at Indiana University, Marty had the opportunity to audition for Les Elgart's Ensemble. Les had begun his career more than twenty years earlier working with jazz legends such as Harry James and Nelson Riddle. Both popular band leaders through the 40's and 50's.

These Jazz pioneers were household names in the years just before rock and roll and the Beatles changed the direction of American music forever. Les' biggest claim to fame however was the musical theme to American Bandstand. A jazz swing hit that played on almost every radio and then television until the 70's. Little did Marty know that this initial audition with Les would lead him to work with these same jazz legends later in his own career.

The audition was another typical band audition, but this wasn't for academics. It could mean his first "professional" tour. Sure, he'd been paid for some individual performances here and there, and the gig with the Four Freshmen was compensated, so technically he was already a pro. But this was the type of opportunity that could launch young Marty on the circuit.

The first step to his goal. Getting this job would mean leaving school and going on the road. The young and naive Mr. Harrell was drawn by the thought of playing key notes for a horn section like the bands on Ed Sullivan and the Tonight Show.

The audition was at the University Hall in Chicago, and it wasn't an open audition as Marty had thought. He had been recommended to Les by one of his musician friends and would be meeting with Les in a more informal setting. The experiences he garnered as pep band leader and then in the University orchestra made him acutely aware of the importance of both his fundamentals of scale and rhythm, but also the presence of performance.

Not only was it important to be technically apt, but stage presence was also a major factor. When the arrangement called for the bass trombone catch phrase, Marty made sure his tone was sharp, and he looked good playing it. It must have worked.

By the end of the audition session, Les looked over at Marty.

"Bass Trombone…. you got the job," he said and went on to the next position. It was not lost on Marty that this menial assignment made by Les Elgart himself, almost in passing, would be the next major step in a career that would have Marty as Bass Trombone for the likes of Sinatra and Elvis Presley—as in the long-term goal he made with Bill Bell's prompting in years previous.

* * *

The tour bus was a big monster of a vehicle, and not necessarily in a good way. Unlike the school buses Marty rode in his youth, this bus had padded seats, windows that worked, a restroom—which stunk of holy hell—and spring shocks like the tractor he drove on the golf course. So, in many ways, it was a dream come true—he was on tour as a professional musician with the Les Elgart Band.

It's just that dreams didn't necessarily include things like the bus's stinking restroom, and the nights of endless driving without a decent bed to sleep in. But he was "on tour." It was a story of success for this Midwestern hometown boy.

One whole section of seats on the bus was reversed with a table in the middle. This was the card table, and this is where Marty learned to play poker, on the long days and nights on the road.

On their first stop outside of Chicago, it was raining and dark. They'd been traveling for several hours and were weary of the beating rain, and diesel exhaust that somehow circulated back into the bus. As they closed in to the Navy NCO club for their tour opener, they were all anxious to get a short stretch and a bite to eat.

On a rainy Midwestern night, the bus driver shot past the turn-off and was forced to attempt a wide U-turn on a dirt farm road. The rain had turned the shoulder into a lake of mud and muck as the bus wound around, sputtered, stopped, then tilted, and spun the inside wheels like a motorboat.

At first the bus driver was confident that he could free the land yacht from the mud lake, but as he tried desperately to move forward, then backward, wheels turned in, then out he finally admitted defeat. They were stuck and would be late for the gig.

Someone would have to hoof it to the nearest phone and call for a heavy-duty tow truck. Luckily, a nearby farmhouse and a late-night tow company would be enroute soon enough. They were scheduled to be at the venue a couple hours early for set up, rehearsal and sound check, so it would be possible to make the gig by show time—they didn't really need to rehearse anyway.

After getting out of the bus for the tow truck rescue, up to their knees in soaked cow patties and red clay, the bus made their sloppy way to the venue and the Les Elgart band hopped it up like no other, mud and stained suits notwithstanding. Marty's glamourous ideals of being on the road had taken a plunge in the mud, but it was no worse for wear.

* * *

As the popularity of American Swing Jazz started to wane in the late 50's with the growing popularity of Rhythm & Blues and nascent Rock & Roller's just breaking into the scene, Les' Jazz Ensemble would continue to tour the Midwest keeping the big band sound alive through the early 60's. Which is just the experience and opportunity Marty needed to catapult him into the Big Band "Big Leagues."

Later that year, while touring with Les' Ensemble, Jeff James, an amazing trumpet player, son of legendary Bandleader Harry James—one of the greatest big band leaders of the 30's and 40's—was invited to a private audition for the Tommy Dorsey Orchestra. Marty and Jeff had been playing together with Les and had become good friends.

Through the previous two decades, Tommy Dorsey and his Orchestra were the essence of the big band sound. They toured the nation for twenty years, popularizing the Swing dance and the Big Band sound. Frank Sinatra, among other entertainment giants of the time, sang with, and toured with the Tommy Dorsey Orchestra. "I'll Never Smile Again" featuring Sinatra and The Pied Pipers held the No. 1 spot on the charts for 12 weeks in 1940 and was Dorsey's biggest hit of all time.

Although the great musician and band leader whose namesake the band held had passed away almost a decade before, his band, led by Sam Donahue, a pioneer of American Swing and Jazz—and an accomplished saxophone player himself, continued to tour the big cities: New York, Chicago, Las Vegas and San Francisco. That's when Sam Donahue and band promoter Tino Barzie envisioned a big band nostalgia tour for the Nevada, California circuit.

Jeff James invited Marty along for the audition to be held at a small music studio in Chicago. He told Marty, "This was an opportunity that could launch his career." Playing with the Tommy Dorsey Orchestra under Sam Donahue would elevate him to the top echelon of musicianship. It would open so many doors into the music industry. Jeff felt, since he was personally "invited" to the audition, he would be a shoo-in for First Trumpet—not to mention his legendary father.

Sam Donahue was bigger than life. He dressed casually and had a certain saunter that betrayed his reputation as the "Sentimental Gentleman of Swing." He had made his name as a jazz saxophonist and trumpeter, but later in his career, as arranger and band leader, his snappy swinging horn riffs and jazz percussion arrangements set teenage feet stomping and shouting just like the golden era of jazz following World War II, where he had conducted the Navy band after Artie Shaw.

Since Marty was really tagging along with Jeff James, he took his place in a corner and hoped to have an opportunity to showcase his own talent. The little music hall was dark and dank. It had the smell of a hundred-year-old theater and a light layer of dust settled over the entire studio stage area. The orchestra sat behind wire music stands and metal chairs—not what Marty had envisioned for the band that had helped create the latest incarnation of Frank Sinatra.

Marty's luck was palpable. He could tell by the spread of the brass that there wouldn't be much competition if any at bass trombone. Within minutes of taking his position near the far left of the horn section the gentlemanly band leader noted the young trombone player. The band's current bass trombonist would be leaving the band before the next tour. The legendary saxophonist motioned over to the nervous young horn player.

"Hey you kid, you play bass trombone? How'd you like to sit in for this session?" he asked.

"Sure," was all that needed to be said. He was handed a stack of sheet music for bass trombone but since this was going to be a nostalgia tour, Marty knew many of the tracks and the swing timing was all too familiar. His parents had been listening to these hits for most of his lifetime—and he knew all the horn parts. Jeff glared at Marty.

By the end of the audition, Sam Donahue told Marty, "You're perfect. We're hitting the road in a week. Get your horns packed."

Jeff was not too pleased. He didn't get picked for First Trumpet. In fact, he didn't even make the Third Trumpet, and that's all the trumpets that were needed for the Tommy Dorsey Orchestra.

* * *

The tour bus was an original of the Tommy Dorsey Orchestra and had been around ever since and looked like it. I was the color of gray diesel exhaust and roadkill, but it was painted "Tommy Dorsey and his Orchestra" in bright blue letters that let everyone on the highway know, that some of the best party starters, horn blowers and swing jazz musicians were on their way to bring young hearts to their stomping and swinging best at their next stop.

Marty recalls the moment he left home to join the band on his first tour. Sam was such a gentleman as he spoke in his most comforting and respectful manner to Marty's mom Eula. Although Marty had been on tour with Les Elgart and was away from home for weeks at a time, she always knew he was not too far away—within the safety and sanctity of the Midwest states.

This tour would take Marty to the West Coast for six months. Sam tried to impress upon her that he personally would be looking out for her son, and that it would be an experience of a lifetime, they were heading to Las Vegas, Los Angeles, and San Francisco, and that "everything would be alright." She cried on Sam's shoulder and hugged Marty tightly for what seemed like five minutes.

Eula said to Sam, "you take care of my boy."

"He should be okay, if we can keep him away from the tables." Sam quipped.

"That will be a problem because he loves to eat!" Marty's mother innocently responded. She didn't know much about the "tables" in Las Vegas!

* * *

Being on tour presented an interesting mix of living out of a bag, carrying your equipment around, eating an eclectic mix of home-style comfort food and dry sandwiches, and playing to a crowd of sweet smelling honeys and sweaty brutes each night before packing up, and loading back on the bus for a short ride, or sometimes a long ride to the next dusty hall.

Life on the road was not as glamorous as in the movies. The bus was big and noisy, smelled of stale diesel and oil (and crap), but it was the paid-for mode of transportation, it was their bus-ride to fame and fortune, it was a way to make a living, and it paid $150 per week.

Since they roomed together, got lots of Happy Hour eats, and drank to their heart's content, the money could go a long way. They literally had neither the time nor opportunity to spend it. Their schedule took them to a different venue and hotel each night. Hours on the road, greasy fast food, setup-gig-tear-down, drink like a fish, maybe get some flirting in, sleep, back on the road…

Memories of those first few months blurred into two- and three-month blocks of the cycle. It was tough at first. It almost reminded Marty of going camping out in the woods, but there was a lot more smoke and they had to dress like a penguin each night and play instruments. Marty was young and it didn't occur to him that this would be a tough existence for a 40-year-old.

He wondered if this is what it was like being with a traveling circus, or even a chain gang—well it could feel that way in some moments.

Race Relations

In high school, Marty was leader of the Pep Band. Although he inherited the leadership role as a sophomore he really organized and promoted their gigs. They would play at all the rallies and basketball games.

His leadership role expanded beyond just FJ Reitz High School; the Pep Band members were also part of the all-city band and orchestra. It was a time and place where the band and orchestra might be as popular as football, where parents, friends and family would attend every event with the same level of enthusiasm.

They would rehearse once a week with all the high schools in the town. As conductor, Marty came to know all the conductors at each high school. In particular, Marty became great friends with the conductor of Central High School—the all-black high school. Naive young Marty never understood why they were in different schools. Although segregation was still de facto, it wasn't spoken about.

In his Senior Year, the same time the Civil Rights movement inflamed the South, Marty and friends came up with the caper to top their year. In the final week of the football season, Marty shared his plan. His pep band would travel to the Central High School and substitute for their pep rally, and the pep band from Central would play at Reitz High School's pep rally.

Marty had proposed the idea to the principal earlier in the year and it was more or less ignored. The principal didn't want to get anywhere near the Civil Right posturing in Evansville, Indiana with any type of inflammatory event.

The plan was made; the stage set without so much as a leak or hiccup. Marty's Pep Band was greatly received, and everyone loved the stunt. In his own way Marty led his own civil rights movement. And he would have more opportunity once the tour headed South.

* * *

In Marty's first season with the Tommy Dorsey Band, an already legendary trumpet player, Charlie Shavers joined the band as featured trumpet. He had been the lead trumpet for a decade through the 40's and 50's.

By the early sixties he was in the twilight of his career having played at one time or another with Frank Sinatra, Dizzy Gillespie and Billie Holiday among a host of other swing era greats.

It was the first Southern swing of the tour where Marty would get his next life lesson in Civil Rights. Despite the segregation in Southern Indiana, Marty wasn't really following the events of the era.

At their first stop after crossing the Mason Dixon line, the bus stopped to check-in in Montgomery, Alabama. It was this first stop where the hotel clerk would not allow Charlie to stay in the white hotel.

"He's gonna have to stay in the black hotel down the way." The clerk said nonchalantly to Sam. The place stank of gutter and sweat, and Marty couldn't believe the man as he spoke to Sam Donahue with no regard of their famous band name and celebrity.

"Then you've lost all our business, we're staying in the bus tonight," was the reply.

Marty never thought about his mark in the history of the Civil Rights era, but the statement would be made, time and time again. And Marty could always take solace in the fact that he was on the right side of that debate.

Exchange Band

In January of 1964, the Tommy Dorsey band, with Frank Jr. as headliner, was scheduled for a three-week United Kingdom tour which would include the Odeon and the New Victoria theatres in London. What Marty and band did not realize was that the arrangement they were fulfilling was to create a scheduling gap in their US tour schedule, which could allow another act to fill the gaps at those venues.

In essence, they were being scheduled as an "exchange" band. The concept was to keep the tour schedule locked up in America while they took the band overseas. British promoters would work with their American counterparts so that they would keep the venues busy while the domestic band went overseas—sort of a prisoner exchange. So while the Tommy Dorsey Orchestra was making a circuit of England, a British band would fill in the schedule in the American circuit.

These types of exchanges were more or less informal and there's not much documentation to support a formal exchange program, but it can be verified that the Tommy Dorsey Orchestra was scheduled for several stops in London in January through February of 1964. It was a grueling pace. The orchestra played eighteen nights in eighteen different theatres around London between February 1st and the 29th.

No one in the band thought there might be some underlying agenda to the British tour, but the Tommy Dorsey Orchestra would be overseas at the same moment as the first shot across the pond of the "British Invasion." The most famous live debut on the Ed Sullivan Show occurred while the Tommy

Dorsey Orchestra was slinging the best of American swing and jazz at the Odeon Southend Theatre in London.

On that same night in CBS Studio 50 in New York City, the Ed Sullivan Show would be hosting the following guests: the Cast of "Oliver!," Impressionist/Comedian Frank Gorshin aka the Riddler, and an innovative new rock and roll band from England.

When they returned from their three-week circuit, all Marty and Frank Jr. would hear about for the next several months was this new four-man band, with electric guitars, a distinctive new sound, with long hair and crazy outfits. The band they were playing in exchange for? None other than the Beatles. And it would set into motion a decades-long shift in the whole landscape of popular music and the music and entertainment industry as a whole.

Marty might call it the end of the Big Band era.

The Camera Bug

While in Frankfurt, the boys were hanging around before the evening show taking in the historical grounds and more recent WWII ruins throughout the countryside. Although both knew plenty of the textbook history of the war in Europe and the American involvement, they were impossibly disconnected from the human devastation and destruction of war.

Nothing could tell the tale like standing next to a pile of rubble, that was once clearly a thousand-year-old building. Rubble that more than likely saw the blood and fallen bodies of soldiers and civilians alike. He could imagine many of the soldiers on all sides of the war were young men his age. It was one of the most sobering and life-changing memories of Marty's young life.

But there were also the curious times enjoyed by many naive travelers from the West. As a shutterbug, Frank Jr. had been told by his father about the best store for German cameras and lenses—and it was in Frankfurt. Frank Jr. would take Marty along just as best buddies would. Marty, however, never had the extra dough to afford such extravagant items, but hanging out with Frank Jr. always led to interesting adventures.

The proprietor of this particular camera shop in Frankfurt was a personal friend of Frank Sr. and was supposedly able to get Frank Jr. the best equipment for the best price—guaranteed.

After a light lunch and before rehearsal, Frank and Marty jumped into a cab and told the driver to take them to "Haake & Albers on Große

Bockenheimer Straße" he said reading it off a paper—neither Frank Jr. nor Marty spoke a lick of German. It was a little rainy and cold this February afternoon in '64 and the boys didn't have time to take an exploratory walk in the rain.

The two needed to be back at the Alte Oper (Old Opera) Concert Hall for 2pm rehearsal. Glancing at their watches as the driver took turn after turn and seemed to take forever to get to what they thought was the "local" camera store. Frank Jr. was surprised by the cab fare, but they had little choice but to keep to their schedule and be sure to allow enough time for the return trip.

The old Haake & Albers Camera Store was the true portrait of irony. It had clearly been around for many years and lacked a woman's touch. The display shelves were dusty and in disarray but there was a lab and work area behind a counter that was immaculate.

The wet boys brought in a musty damp smell as they wiped their shoes on the mat trying not to make too much of a commotion. They could detect the smell of glass cleaner, light jewelry oil, and floating dust-balls that effectuated the science-lab-like ambiance.

Of course, this wasn't going to be a quick transaction. Frank Jr. was looking to spend several hundred American dollars on a Hasselblad body and a set of lenses that would support his photo-buggery. With less than a half-hour until rehearsal, Marty urged Frank to finish up.

"We're not going to make it back for tune-up," Marty urged. Sam Donahue ran a tight ship, and the second most strident disciplinarian was

Frank Jr. himself. It would not make for good appearances if they showed up late. And based on the ride there, they were going to be 20 minutes late, plus a stop at their room at the Hilton 5 minutes away to grab Marty's horns. At least Frank could go directly there. Marty would be at least 30 minutes late.

"Frank, we've got to go, Sam will have our hides," Marty was apoplectic. The shopkeeper was the picture of grace under pressure, "where do you boys need to be? The Hilton or the Alte Opre?"

"We need to be back at the Hilton Frankfurt and then to the Alte Opre by 2 o'clock. We'll never make it."

"Relax" he said in his clearest Germanically accented English, "it's a five-minute walk up Goethepl street."

The Vegas Club, Dallas, Texas

One of the more popular nightclubs in Dallas, Texas in the 50's and into the 60's was called the Vegas Club. This popular venue, which was a dance club but also would feature striptease, was owned by a well-known Texas bar and night club owner, Jack. During the spring of 1963 (before Frank Jr's kidnapping), the Tommy Dorsey Orchestra was making its way through Dallas and other Texas cities. The Vegas club was one of the stops.

Although a small nightclub that typically hosted local Rhythm & Blues combos and lounge acts like Trini Lopez and Joe Johnson, Jack had booked the Big Band in an effort to bring in bigger names. Marty and the band were a little disappointed at first, they were used to playing in larger concert halls and theatre venues.

They unloaded their gear in front of the club on a paved but dusty parking lot. Once inside they began to assemble their stands for the orchestra seating area. This always took time and Tino would direct the local laborers like an orchestra conductor Everyone was in charge of their instruments. Marty, or anyone else, didn't want any laborer's paws on the tools of their trade.

The Vegas club wasn't really a great venue. The stage was barely big enough for the whole band to fit with chairs, stands, and room for the conductor and Frank Jr. He needed a fairly large area to move around and belt out the tunes, as well as interact with the crowd, it was all part of the show. The band had dealt with these conditions before, and they would make do for their short stint at this nondescript strip-bar like they always did.

But it wasn't this dingy dirty night-club that was so unique—they'd played at dozens of dumps just as dingy and dirty. This place was a little sketchier because of the mobsters who seemed to be regulars there. You couldn't, or wouldn't, look them in the eye. If you did, you felt a chill running up your spine like you might not make it out of there alive.

Eva was the club manager, and she bossed everyone around as if she were the Godfather—but she did run a tight ship. Apparently, Eva's brother Jack owned the place for over a decade. Jack was a seasoned tough guy/bar owner. He was a 50's-ish, round-bodied, balding, wanna-be big-shot, but under the cheap suit was a former weightlifter and boxer, who loved a good barroom brawl.

He was the typical type of character that results from hard nights drinking and dealing with the 2am dregs. He was brash but fun and assured Sam he would be able to attract a full house for the show.

He and Eva welcomed the boys with open arms and an open bar tab. The Vegas club may have been a hole-in-the-wall compared to some of the other clubs back East, but the owner and the hometown Dallas crowd was a party to be had. The few gigs they did at the Vegas club were a smash. The band played for packed houses each night and the strippers didn't make their appearance till much later in the evening once the good girls had gone home.

Later that year, following several Midwestern and Northeastern tours, the orchestra headed for Lake Tahoe. It was, November 22nd, two-weeks before the kidnapping of Frank Jr. The band members were finishing up a rehearsal when Charlie Shavers came to Marty. Normally cool and the picture of smooth, Charlie was distraught like Marty had never seen him before. He looked like he was in shock. He had tears in his eyes, and his hands trembled.

"President Kennedy has been shot!" Charlie Shavers, Marty and several of the band members gathered around a transistor radio to listen to the live broadcast. The voice of Walter Cronkite came over the crackly speaker. Details were vague but JFK had been visiting Dallas, where the band had toured earlier in that season. Early descriptions of the shooter and many other confusing reports flew through the airwaves.

Everyone was shocked. Many were walking around like zombies, staring into space, sobbing, wondering what could possibly be the worst—would the president survive? Within the next hour, amidst the fear, uncertainty and confusion, Cronkite would declare that the doctors at Parkland Hospital in Dallas had declared the president had died.

Many of the black musicians of the band had very strong affection for the Civil Rights advocate. Their dreams of a new integrated country had come to a screeching halt. Someone had assassinated John F. Kennedy.

Not much more could be done. They were finishing their tour and heading back to Vegas, where they would take a one-week respite and then go on a winter tour starting in the Southwest, Los Angeles, then to Reno and Tahoe. Tonight, the show did go on. But no one was quite themselves, the country had changed. A communist named Lee Harvey Oswald had been captured and allegedly was the one who shot Kennedy from a sixth-floor window above Dealey Plaza.

The next day more details would emerge about Oswald, the rifle found, his family and the successful assassination. It wasn't until the following day, November 24th, that another earth-shattering news report hit the airwaves. Jack Ruby had shot Lee Harvey Oswald in the basement of Dallas PD headquarters on the way to his arraignment. Once again, the news shot through the airwaves as the Kennedy saga took another unexpected turn. The owner of the Vegas club, Jack Ruby, was now also an integral part of our Nation's tragic history.

The South American Tour June 1965

Marty had only heard of Rio de Janeiro and Peru in stories and songs like "Come Fly with Me." These far off destinations were the subject of tales and music that brought the bossa-nova and samba rhythms that cause hips to gyrate like no other rhythm before it. Now the whole of the Tommy Dorsey Orchestra were on an airplane to go to the most exotic lands Marty could imagine in his young career. The boys and their band leader were off on a charter non-stop from New York to Buenos Aires, Argentina.

Before taking off from New York to Buenos Aires just after the air crew finished locking up the cabin door, the pilot came to the front of the plane for an announcement. This was not typical but then Marty hadn't flown to South America before. He had known from listening to the daily news that the countries they would be touring were also a hotbed of political unrest—but those stories never hit home for Midwestern Marty—until now. There was the Cuba/Russian thing still lingering. And all kinds of news out of Mexico City and Argentina. Exactly where they were headed.

Now the captain, dressed in his uniform and captain's hat, stood in the front of the cabin waiting to get everyone's attention. Finally, they got everyone quiet and the pilot began. He was dead serious—he didn't look like he was going to read the dinner menu.

"As this is a commercial charter, the State Department has advised that travel to several South American countries is not advised. Political unrest in Argentina, Peru, Ecuador and Brazil has destabilized the region with anti-American sentiment and travel is considered high-risk for

Americans. Because of the status of your tour and some of the members of your band, he looked over at Frank Jr., it might be considered a target for bombing or kidnapping.

"The State Department has been in communication with Interpol and agents will be meeting us at the airport and accompanying the band during the tour. Because the band is a high-profile American entertainment company and the American government is considered pro-resistance by some of these countries, individuals will not be allowed to travel separately from the tour group."

Well, that was food for thought as they buckled their seat belts and prepared for what could only be an adventure of a lifetime.

"I guess we're not going to Machu Pichu!" Marty quipped to Frank.

Flying in the 1960's was much different compared to the structured and rigid air travel phenomenon we experience today. The planes seemed loud and rickety and at high altitudes, although the cabins were pressurized, there was always a little lightheadedness and a sense of disaster pending at every yaw and pitch.

Add a little highball into the mix and all the second-hand smoke and the high-flyer would discover what Frank Sr. was singing about "rarified air" and being "starry eyed."

Landing in this strange land of the Southern Hemisphere, Marty recalls the quaint, smoky towns that were vaguely reminiscent of pictures of European cities surrounded by third-world shantytowns like what he'd seen traveling to Mexico. Streetside cafes, late dinners, the sound of kids screaming, singing and car horns filling in the gaps. Sometimes the sound of gunfire.

Like most of the third world, it seemed there were only very poor people, and very rich people. Very different from the middle-class suburbia, the Great Plains, and big city sprawl that the young American was more accustomed to. Most of the poor seemed to be of more indigenous peoples, shorter, darker skin, hard callused hands and dark eyes with drawn expressions—eyes turned down.

The rich could have been models and society elite of any modern Western or European country, tall, slender, bejeweled, with that lighter shade of skin-tone—tanned, not from outdoor labor, and the high cheekbones and animated expressions that reminded Marty of the Roaring 20's and the Great Gatsby. They had their drivers, bodyguards and servants like Marty had also not seen in America. Grab a cigarette, and it was a competition for which clerk, waiter, or maître d' would offer the flame first.

The modern people with their many languages and dialects still all sounded the same to his Southern Indianan ears. Marty's most odd but interesting recollection was of the cars. Although a whole generation and a half older—the roads were clogged with 1930's and 1940's era American cars—they were all in pristine shape—as if they'd just been driven off the lot last year. It was like a twilight zone trip back in time—war time.

Buenos Aires would be the first stop of Marty's South American tour with the Tommy Dorsey Orchestra. The head-spinning schedule was packed with sold-out shows at some of the largest soccer stadiums, bull-fighting rings, and opera houses of the proud South American countries they'd be visiting.

Add to that recipe for volatility, the fact that many of the countries were in so much political turmoil that almost any random last-minute event might cause a cancellation. This happened once in Peru, where the Junta made a move on the President and locked down the airport from international flights. The show, in that case, would not go on.

In another incident in Quito, Ecuador, Tino took one look at the "Opera House" and proclaimed, "there's no rear exit, we can't play here." Tino Barzie was the orchestra's road manager through most of the 1960's. Not only was he responsible for logistics and travel arrangements, but he was also responsible for the band's safety and security.

They were booked to play the stadium in Buenos Aires, their opener, then they would cross the bay to Montevideo, Uruguay for a gig the following night. Each night was sold out but the weather and travel arrangements weren't what the big band was accustomed to traveling in the US.

A dense fog over Buenos Aires delayed their landing. The fog hadn't lifted by day two and they could not open the runways to make the short flight to Montevideo, Uruguay. But they had to make the show, it was sold out and would be their only stop in the country, possibly ever. Their options were to take a ferry, or board a bus for the 6-hour slog around the bay.

The best possible transport across Rio de La Plata Bay at that time would be by ferry. But it wasn't a regular flat ferry boat like back home.

This one was a mixture of a modern steel-hulled, streamlined ship and a 1800's era riverboat, because it was propelled by a giant paddle-wheel—as big as the multi-storied ship itself. Something one might think they'd see in a modern European country—not necessarily in Argentina—but what did Marty know?

Filled with a mixture of tourists, Argentinians and indigenous natives, the ferry rocked and rolled along with the waves in a constant stomach-churning pendulum motion. It might not have been so bad but the heavy fog laying over the bay made for very little reference or scenery. Plus, it was the middle of the night so only the lights from the ferry and the shimmering dots off the coastal cities overlaid with the heavy mist made for a most serene ambiance.

Marty recalls looking over the rails of the giant ferry, at this enormous wood and metal wheel, cranking away, four hours to Montevideo. They would arrive well past midnight.

But the trip wasn't so bad, there was a bar on board. Which provided a great opportunity for the band members to pass the time.

As they disembarked the ferry and were lined up checking through customs, they did their head count, and they were one short. A short pause, discussions, and somebody proclaimed, "It's Charlie, Charlie Shavers is missing."

"Check the bar, that's the last place I saw him," proclaimed Marty. Sure enough, Charlie Shavers had fallen asleep on one of the bar lounges.

After the show at the packed Antel Arena, it was once again time to cross the bay and record a television show first thing in the morning. Then they were scheduled to catch a flight to Rio de Janeiro. But the fog persisted, and the runways stayed closed.

This time they didn't have all night to travel with the natives on the big ferry. Their studio schedule was for 6am and the band needed to get some rest before taping a live show.

Tino Barzie once again sprang to action. It was a good thing that money wasn't an issue. Where there is cash there is a way. Hydrofoil. Marty and the band had never seen anything like this contraption except in James Bond movies. It was a very sleek and futuristic-looking boat, possibly a catamaran. But there were some mysterious powerhouses rumbling and gurgling below deck.

They cruised smoothly and silently from the pier when everyone, and their horns were on board. But once they got out of the harbor, the captain punched it and the hydrofoil planes would raise the boat's hull about 5 feet out of the water and go real fast. The vehicle was not as big as the ferry, but all 30 of the band members, singers, roadies and guides were seated comfortably and in less than half the time and swells, they arrived at their hotel rooms and got at least a few hours of shuteye before the taping.

The next morning, they traveled by bus to the El Trece (Channel 13) television studio in Buenos Aires. Bleary-eyed and many going without breakfast, just a cup of coffee (great coffee by the way) the Tommy Dorsey Orchestra organized themselves for a live broadcast that would be shown on local television.

Marty wondered just how many televisions there actually were in Argentina in 1963. He'd be surprised to discover that much like the US, almost 92% of Argentinian households had televisions.

About halfway through the set, Frank jr. was right in the middle of "Come Fly with Me" and singing about llama land, when the Interpol agent brusquely opened up the studio door—while the red "ON THE AIR" sign was lit brightly—so it must have been important, and said, "We've got to get back to the hotel."

"What's going on?" Asked thirty-plus musicians at the same time.

"There's a report that a group is coming to the studio to stage an Anti-American protest. Time to go. Get your instruments and make an orderly line to exit out the back of the studio. Agent Perez will lead the way. We have several vans and jeeps parked around back, get on one and get back to your room at the hotel. DO NOT SEPARATE FROM THE GROUP."

"Where's the bus?" Someone asked obviously.

"We can't take the bus. It would be an obvious target. Get into the vans in groups of five or six. The rest can get on the jeeps. They'll be leaving out the back separately."

The women cried and many of the men were very nervous, but they knew how to follow simple instructions. As they made a line outside behind the studio and started loading into the various vehicles glommed together by the local police and the few Interpol agents, things seemed to be progressing in an orderly fashion.

That's when a roar of angry Argentinians ran up to the front of the studio building and rocks started hitting the front windows of the studio in loud crashes, some people started smashing doors and coming into the studio. There was a lot of shouting and crashing of glass when Marty made a beeline, trombone case in hands, to the back exit right behind Frank.

Marty and Frank were among the last in the line out the door just clearing the back exit when the destruction began. Forget orderly! Now they sprinted out the back and looked for a jeep or van that was supposed to be waiting for them. Frank Jr. was several steps in front of Marty (he didn't have a giant horn case) and jumped on the back of the army jeep in a nick of time as the jeep started out the gate.

Marty, lugging this big black bass trombone case, felt like he was carrying a dead body—head still bleary from the late-night travel and snooze. He was losing ground to the jeep that was accelerating while Frank shouted at the driver to stop—he wasn't listening to Frank though.

As Marty took a couple of desperate steps with all his effort to catch up he flung the trombone case like a quarterback, tossing the option to Frank who completed the reception and threw it over his shoulder into the front of the jeep so he could grab Marty.

With renewed energy and spring Marty strode the last few steps unhindered by the unwieldy travel case and grabbed the tailgate of the jeep. Frank grappled with Marty as he dragged his feet for about twenty yards getting aboard. The studio was burned to the ground.

They seemed to be safe at the hotel, but many people from the angry crowds followed in their little cars and motorcycles, while others seemed to already know where they were staying.

Their instructions were to get your stuff and meet back at the hotel entrance. They'd be leaving for the airport as soon as they loaded the bus. As they got to their rooms and started packing their bags in a bum's rush, their room phone rang, "get down to the bus we're leaving NOW." They needed to get out of the hotel before the crowd got too big and raucous. At the hotel entrance army soldiers had gathered out front fully armed with M-16s and full riot gear.

They had surrounded the bus and hotel doors securing a safe passage to board the bus, but they had to get out of town immediately. As the crowd grew, there was no telling how long they would be secure. Luckily, they all made it out and to the airport without further incident, just a few cuts, scrapes and lots of frayed nerves.

1964 World Series

Growing up in Southern Indiana, Marty had a typical Midwestern upbringing. Big on sports and his music, he was also involved in fishing, skiing and golf. However, since there were no professional sports teams in the local area, Marty had never been to a professional sports event.

On their New York swing through New England, the Tommy Dorsey Orchestra was hired to play the introduction and National Anthem for the 1964 World Series. The bandstands were set up on the infield and a small stage was placed opposite the pitcher's mound for Sam to conduct.

As they walked out onto the field, Marty was in awe. He had never seen a venue so large, packed with over 70,000 screaming fans, preparing to watch the Yankees try to beat the St. Louis Cardinals in their fifth World Series meeting.

The excitement was heavy in the air, and the crowd noise made it almost impossible to hear their own instruments. The echo would be dampened by the crowd noise, but they played as professionals do, and they sounded great!

His first professional sports event he would attend would be the fifth game of the 1964 World Series, and he was on the field.

Tony Martin, the celebrity actor and singer, was to perform the National Anthem at this game. Although they'd never performed together, the anthem was a standard that they could play in their sleep. As he walked onto the field for the performance, he wore his trademark straw hat with a dark band. But he removed it for the song and held it in front of his body.

Marty assumed that it was out of respect for the song and flag. But Marty had to chuckle when he spied a sheet of paper stuffed inside the brim. He could just see inside the hat the words, "Oh say can you see…"

* * *

Bass trombone is always on the far stage-left, so on this day, Marty sat on his chair at the edge of the orchestra of the makeshift bandstand. As they started pumping out the tune, Marty could see two shadows standing next to him. Of course, he stayed focused on this sheet music and Sam at the head of the band conducting. Once the number was over, he took a look over his left shoulder, and standing there was none other than Mickey Mantle and Roger Maris.

They stood there while the band played and admired the trombonist and the overall arrangement. Marty could barely hear the band over the roar of the crowd which seemed to lay a low rumble over the entire stadium. During the first break, the two ball players walked over to Marty and asked about the interesting looking brass instrument.

The two hit it off and this first encounter would be the beginning of a long friendly relationship as Mickey was a huge fan of the big band sound.

In later years, Mickey would follow the Tommy Dorsey band and catch their performances when they were in New York, front and center. Mickey, in his big self, was low-key and loved to tap his heels and snap his fingers to the swing and bossa-nova beats.

At the end of the performances, Marty would help Mickey, bad knees and all, up on to the stage to take a few bows. Of course, the crowds would go wild. Then he'd exit out the service entrance backstage so he could disappear and avoid the crowd. Although never a close relationship, it was one that lasted many years.

4th of July Mayhem

Being part of a musical ensemble brings people of many different backgrounds together. Taking them on tour for weeks at a time, and they get to know each other very intimately. People get to know each other in ways they might never know, but for sitting in a bus together for hours on end.

Marty and his bandmates were always messing with each other and searching for a laugh. Whether it was hanging with Charlie Shavers, messing with the band manager Tino Barzie (always a great target for ball busting) or just a little ribbing or hazing between the horn section and the rest of the band, someone was always looking to outdo the last prank and the band was a reliable captive audience to use and abuse while on the road.

Frank Jr. was not an innocent bystander. Sometimes the son of a legend could get away with more than the regular Joe, but Frank didn't consider himself special, he was just as capable and likely to be the pranker or pranked.

On a hot summer weekend, just before the 4th of July holiday, the tour was at the local hotel for the weekend shows. Across and down the street from the hotel was a fireworks shack with big 4th of July specials. Frank decided that some roman candles and cherry bombs would be a good investment for the weekend's adventures.

Marty and Frank Jr. had just finished inventorying their armament (fireworks) in the hotel room when they decided they were ready for a gag. What could be better than a cherry bomb in an elevator? The two started riding the elevators up and down waiting for a good potential victim, when at the top of the hotel, the doors opened up to Tino, who was heading down to the lobby for a bite to eat.

The boys politely greeted Tino and stepped out of the elevator on one side so Tino could then get in. As they switched places and turned facing each other, the doors were about to close—Frank Jr. deftly slides a round red cherry bomb from his pocket, lights it with his Zippo, and tosses it onto the floor of the elevator just before the doors slowly shut. They could hear a muffled, "Hey, you f……" then—BOOM! Just as the elevator started descending.

"Did you see the look on his face?" Marty was crouched over laughing.

"I think he's going to be pissed at me!" Frank proclaimed proudly as they pushed the elevator down button and made more plans for another stunt.

Little did they know that the cherry bomb blew a hole through Tino's pants and lower leg leaving a large open wound with paper and fireworks debris mixed in the blood and torn clothing—it was actually a major injury that needed medical attention.

Tino hobbled out of the elevator and fell to the floor shouting for help. One of the other band members that was in the lobby rushed Tino to the emergency room for treatment. Frank was right—Tino was PISSED.

Upon getting back to the hotel, Frank and Marty couldn't be more apologetic. They had no idea the cherry bomb would wreak so much havoc and injury to Tino, and they truly felt bad—for several minutes anyway.

Frank apologized sincerely but Tino would have none of it. Tino was so angry at Frank that it didn't take too long for him to once again become the butt of Frank's jokes as he limped around in cast and crutches playing the victim, cursing and verbally abusing the boys at will.

Luckily, Tino had plenty of painkillers to ease the pain and help him sleep. Tino was mostly done for this part of the tour anyway and could relax in his room while the band finished this last gig before heading home.

Back on the tour bus for a midnight ride, Tino could only sit at the front of the bus. His wrapped and throbbing leg needed to be elevated and the only seat that allowed it was the very front seat facing the steps that descended to the door. There Tino could lay back and prop his damaged limb on the guardrail. Past midnight most of the band were either asleep or resting quietly as the bus rumbled and bungled down the road.

One of the non-sleepers was Charlie Shavers. Charlie always sat at the back of the bus where he could enjoy his favorite pastime which didn't involve blowing into a horn. Rather he liked breathing in a special type of smoke from a non-labeled cigarette.

Charlie always opened the last two rows of windows to get a breeze going that could circulate the smoke of his stash and try to balance the foul stench coming from the bus restroom that didn't work and smelled like it.

Late into the evening, Charlie had to relieve himself, and even he would never go into the dungeon of horrific affliction that was the bus "restroom." Finding a paper cup thrown to the side, Charlie did his best to keep everything in the cup. Now what to do with it? The bus windows only came down about 4 inches, no way to get the cup and urine out the window without tipping the cup over.

Reluctantly, Charlie got up and started making his way forward to dump the cup and its warm but rancid contents out the door. His own instability due to being under the influence, and the pitch and yaw of the bus on the road made for an awe-inspiring tight rope walk up the bus center aisle.

Most of the band continued sleeping as Charlie ambled forward balancing the cup like a vaudevillian acrobat, he would lean or hang onto innocent band members lining the aisle unaware of his toxic deed.

Marty happened to be awakened by Charlie's worried complaints, although it was really him muttering to himself as he made his way forward, the loud drone of the bus engine and the tires tearing down the asphalt. Marty watched with one eye open as he thought something spectacular must be about to happen, what with Charlie walking the full length of the bus with a paper cup full of warm urine.

As he approached the front of the bus, Charlie steadied himself, holding on to the seat posts lining the bus aisle with one hand while gently holding the cup of urine in the other. It wasn't so difficult to steady himself; the challenge was to keep hold of the cup without squeezing and crushing it.

As he reached the end of the aisleway just behind the driver, Charlie yelled above the rumble and roar of the giant vehicle bounding down the road for the driver to open the door.

"Hey Max. Open the door." Yelled Charlie.

"What?" The driver turned to look over his shoulder. As he did so, the bus swerved, just a little offline. Nothing that the bus driver couldn't correct in the next heartbeat. But the swerve and dip caused Charlie Shavers to lose his grip on the seatback that he had been holding to steady himself. The bus rocked right. As Charlie tried to catch his balance, he unexpectedly squeezed the cup in his right hand and the warm urine exploded out the top of the cup and drenched the innocent, heavily-sedated Tino Barzie's gauze-wrapped leg.

What happened next can only be described as Webster's unabridged definition of FREAK OUT. Tino freaked out. He started screaming and ranting at Charlie, at the Bus Driver to get him to a hospital, at the others close by to help him take off the bandages, at Frank who was laughing his ass off—the villain in this affair. It was the freak out of the century.

As one of the female assistants came to help Tino, she realized that the thick layers of bandages were soaked in the blood and urine of two different men. It was bedlam and hysterical laughter all at once.

The excitement crescendoed with Tino declaring at the top of his lungs in exasperation, "YOU'RE ALL FIRED!" Which of course led to more laughter and chaos.

Jack Jones meets Frank Jr.

On their circuit through Atlantic City, Frank Jr. wanted to check out a new talent who was topping the Billboard charts. Jack Jones had the flair and mellow vocal cords that could mesmerize any crowd. By the time the Tommy Dorsey Orchestra made its Northeast run to New York and New Jersey, Jack and his most recent Grammy award winning song "Wives and Lovers" was pushing for number 1 in the Top 10.

On this sweep, Marty and the rhythm and horn section of the band was playing in the lounge of the Caesars Atlantic City while Jack Jones was in the showroom of the 500 Club. Marty and Frank Jr., all of 20 years old, found some seats at a booth in the showroom and were preparing to take in Jones' act. Although Frank Jr. was nowhere near as recognizable as his father, anyone who knew anything about the business knew Frank Jr. on sight.

Jack Jones suddenly appeared from backstage and approached the two boys tentatively and stood politely by the two boys waiting for them to finish their discussion. He was in his white dinner jacket looking prim and proper getting ready for his big show.

"Mr. Sinatra," Jack Jones—Grammy Award Winner—practically bowed in his presence. "I'm so honored to meet you." Marty and Frank Jr. were taken a little by surprise and stood up in order to greet him properly.

"I am such a big fan of your father, in fact, I hope to one day work with him. Please offer him my best regards. I hope I didn't disrupt your conversation."

"It's great meeting you, Mr. Jones," Both Marty and Frank greeted him politely and respectfully as they had both been raised. He finished and shuffled humbly away. Marty looked at Frank Jr. and had to stifle a loud guffaw lest Jack Jones might be embarrassed to hear their laughter as he ducked backstage.

Dinner with the Sinatra's

While the mainstream music scene in 1964 being dominated by rock 'n' roll and the British Invasion, there was still a strong touring circuit for big bands, particularly for ballrooms, supper clubs, Las Vegas lounges. Although no longer topping the charts, the demand for the renown orchestra featuring the name of long-passed Tommy Dorsey was still a major attraction.

Touring with the top Big Band was a great way to see the country. The tour routes would make stops at any town or city that was worth noting. Oftentimes Marty didn't know where they were or where they would be the next night.

Whenever they played near New Jersey, Frank Jr. would call this grandmother's house. It was a plain two-story brick building on 415 Monroe St., Hoboken. Invariably, he and Marty would be invited to dinner at the Sinatra home. It became a regular event and could happen for several nights in a row, as long as they were within a cab ride away.

At first, Marty was in awe sitting and eating where the legendary Frank Sinatra was born and raised. A huge Italian spread would always welcome Frank Jr. and his band-mates. Grandma Dolly and Marty, a fireman and one-time prize-fighter, would host the event in the basement. Family friends Jilly and Ed Pucci would be typical guests.

The boys would take a cab from the hotel over to Hoboken, where they were always greeted by the wonderful aromas of garlic bread, spaghetti and the biggest juiciest meatballs Marty had ever tasted. On other nights it was pizza pie and fried chicken. But the red wine always flowed and great time was always had by all.

It was curious that Marty had gotten to know Frank Jr. and his grandparents but had yet to meet the "Chairman of the Board." This legendary moment was not far off.

The Rat Pack—The Sands Hotel

During these tours in 1963-4, the Tommy Dorsey orchestra was playing regularly in Vegas. The Frontier, Sands, Caesar's and Aladdin hotels were the new mecca of nightlife for the West Coast getaways. With the Rat Pack reaching their height of popularity, Frank, Dean and Sammy Davis Jr. would have nightly appearances at 8pm and 12 pm at the Sands. This schedule was great for Frank Jr. and Marty to catch these nightly acts between their own 10pm and 2am performances. That was one of the advantages of being the son of the headliner.

The Count Basie Orchestra was conducted by Quincy Jones, and the two boys would always be hanging out backstage as if they were in the show too. This is the first time Marty would get to meet the legend Frank Sr., along with the illustrious Rat Pack. Frank Sr. would loathe the name. During this time, they referred to themselves as The Klan although Sammy wasn't too keen on the name because of the obvious racial connotations.

There was no missing a hit. Frank had the chart-toppers, and the standard tunes couldn't miss. Dean Martin and his melodic tenor could lull any man or woman with a few beverages as lubrication to an isotonic trance of singing, dancing and laughter. The sound of the full orchestra could do nothing short of overtaking each partying soul with swing and sway.

When the boys were together there were no scripts, lines or plans. The most sophisticated planning was the set-list, and this was decided on by Frank and the conductor and then thrown out the window as the banter came loose. Imitations and long setups broke up the timing. Cigarettes and Jack Daniels were the classy form for the tuxedoed crew.

Although the Rat Pack, as they were popularly known, played a drinking, partying bunch, they weren't profane or illicit. Their hilarious banter was about innuendo and wit. It was an innocent yet addictive pitter patter of what could be and should be and can't be, unless you were one of the Rat Pack themselves. Their comedy was light and pure fun. Jokes tended to be womanizing and alcoholic excess but stopped short at the pun. It was a form of comedy that has yet to return to today's less pure, and virtuous comedy themes.

Playing in a live orchestra behind these syncopated comedy geniuses was an art in itself. Something completely untraditional for most performance swing and big bands of the era. Instead of a light intro, or quick comedy bit seasoned with some key phrases and bumps, playing behind the Rat Pack was a Keystone Cops exercise following a seemingly arbitrary joke-line, highlighting the punchlines, without stepping on the come-backs, and being able to start, stop, and start again, any number, at any time, with any singer. The conductor was the key to the delivery, and it was an artform Quincy Jones made tradecraft. The band members had to watch him like a hawk.

It was a new type of talent-fest evolved from the vaudevillian days made up-to-date and cool for the swinging 60's. Instead of a potpourri of obscure talents and scripted anecdotes, unicycles, hula hoops and nose-flutes, the new genre was three- to four- Italian singers (and a single Jewish black man with one eye), sharing drinks, smoking cigarettes and street-talking each other as they knocked out the charts of the season. It was all Vegas, and they could take it on the road or play it at home each night.

Frank's Gems

One of the greatest examples of Frank Sr.'s innate musical talent came from another backstage incident that would probably never be witnessed by anyone but for the fact that Marty's best friend was Frank's son. Hanging out with Frank Jr. anywhere was always sure to be filled with unexpected fun and excitement.

On this day between rehearsal and their evening show, Frank Sr. was keeping busy filming Rat Pack movies during the day, and doing the Sand's and sometimes Caesar's at night. A hectic schedule for anyone, but this was Frank's second or third re-making of himself and the movies were great fun and huge money makers.

Marty and Frank Jr. were hanging out at the set of Frank's latest film project "Robin and the Seven Hoods." They were just hanging around off the edge of the cameras when Bill Miller, Frank's pianist at the time, came over and handed Frank some sheet music.

"Here's the song you'll be signing for the movie." Bill handed Frank the lead music and Bill sat down at the piano with the piano arrangement. The boys wandered over to the piano to see the master at work.

After a few seconds reviewing the sheet music and mouthing the words, throwing out some pitches and pauses, Bill Miller came in with, "1..2..3..4.." He played the intro and Frank came in exactly on time and in tune.

He sang it perfectly and beautifully as if he were singing a lullaby. Both Frank Jr. and Marty were in awe. Frank Sinatra had never heard the song before, yet he sang it like the world-class crooner he was. Full command of pitch, volume, inflection and vibrato.

Frank Sinatra was more than a wonderful talent. Backstage he was a wonderful human being. He respected every musician in his band. He had the innate understanding that his good performance and good fortune was tightly tied to theirs. He felt the best way to reflect that was through mutual respect.

Yes, the back-and-forth onstage could be trashy and off-color, but he truly loved his backing orchestra. One of the ways he would connect with them during their limited time together was just before rehearsals. Frank would show up promptly several minutes before the official start time when everyone was sure to be there, but before the conductor waved his magic wand to get everyone in time, Frank would take a few minutes to share some of his gems.

The gems were little stories or feelings Frank may have had coursing through his veins at that very moment, and he felt that opening up a little to his captive audience helped to put them at ease. Of course, his gems were not like the more common man. If you or I had a gem of a story to tell, it might be about one of my friends, or maybe a celebrity sighting, or just a funny story. Frank's gems invariably included a celebrity, politician, beautiful movie actress or national event.

* * *

This little gem of a story told by Frank was often repeated to open one of his standards, but it was the day the news broke, and the first time Frank told the story that Marty remembers most.

Frank was about the coolest customer in town. Nothing ruffled his feathers, and all was happy and gay. But in one rehearsal Frank walked in giddy as a schoolboy with a new football. Frank had just got off the phone with NASA mission control and he was informed that the official "wake up" song to greet the Apollo 10 astronauts this morning was "Come Fly with Me!"

It was an honor Frank truly valued, and it became a gem that he used to introduce the song often to the enjoyment of the audience.

Dino's Party Crash

This particular morning, Frank came into the rehearsal a little bleary-eyed. Obviously having the look of either hay fever, or a late night out with the boys. It was the latter; however, it was the boys and girls. It started at Dean and Jeanne Martin's Las Vegas home with Frank and Barbara. Dean had invited a couple of other Rat Packers and their spouses/girlfriends and before too long, it was a full house of Vegas celebrities, B-listers, musicians, and hangers-on.

It was a classic Las Vegas elite party and Frank and Dean were the hosts. Of course, Dean had a great stereo system installed throughout the house and as the desert moon rose overhead, so did the size of the crowd and the volume of the music.

Frank and Barbara had been partying along with the rest of the crowd having a great time when Frank was called to the door. It was well past midnight, and the party wasn't slowing down or getting any quieter. Frank wasn't really quite sure why he was being summoned, it wasn't his house.

Outside, in the brisk desert coolness, two Las Vegas PD officers waited politely at the door, both officers clearly sensitive to the fact that despite the fact, that some of the biggest celebrities and their friends were having a bang-up time behind the doors, they still had to serve and protect and get the party under control.

"Mr. Sinatra, we've had a complaint about the loud music, it is past midnight and city ordinance requires that you turn it down. Actually, the caller wanted us to shut the party completely down."

"Really. Ok, you got it." Frank went back into the house and quickly but politely asked everyone to leave. It was late anyway. The crowd expressed their disappointment and began to slowly shuffle out of the house. Some stayed to clean up a bit. Jeanne and Barbara ran around with the trash bags and collected cups and bottles strewn around the house.

Cigarette butts were everywhere. By the time the crowd cleared out and the major junk and trash items picked up and piled them in the sink and dumpster it was well past 1am and Frank and Barbara were ready to head home.

Through all this, Frank had no idea where Dean was. It was his home; he should have been the one to give the "go home" command. He asked the ladies. No one had seen Dean for a while. Frank made his way upstairs to see if everything was okay. Dean's bedroom door was closed.

Frank knocked lightly, not quite knowing what to expect. It could literally be anything behind the door—Dean and Jeanne, a dead body, any of another two or more people getting along behind closed doors, doing whatever they might do with some privacy—anything.

"Yes?" It was Dean's mellow voice, slightly annoyed.

Frank walked in to find Dean in his PJs in bed with a book, his reading glasses tilted down his nose looking up and Frank. He had a slightly crooked smirk on his face.

"Did you just call the cops on your own party?" Frank asked just to get it.

"Well, I was tired." Was all Dino offered.

The Twin Palms

Marty traveled to Palm Springs with Frank Jr. to Frank Sr's house in the mid-sixties. There was a helicopter port in the front driveway. The kitchen and dining room had a table that held about 12 people. The kitchen was as big as a regular house. In the backyard, there was a piano shaped swimming pool and a guest house. It was hexagon shaped and had six apartments.

The house was built for Sinatra and first wife, Nancy Barbato, and featured four bedrooms, a master and one for each of his kids, Nancy, Frank Jr., and Tina. The property, which the Klan would refer to as "Twin Palms" featured a flagpole between two large palm trees, which rumor had that Frank Sr. would hoist a Jack Daniels flag to announce it was cocktail hour and those who knew the meaning were welcome to join in the revelry. Some of his famous neighbors like Bob Hope, Bing Crosby, Al Jolson, Jack Benny, and Cary Grant would stop by to share a cocktail and some eats.

There was an office/den area filled with Emmys, Grammys and Gold Records, more frames, awards and pictures of Frank with only the most celebrated of his crew. Frank with JFK. Frank with world leaders. Frank with the Pope. Frank with Elvis. Other memorabilia, and of course the Oscar. The Academy Award Frank had won for From Here to Eternity sat on a shelf in all its glory in front of Marty and pal.

For Frank Jr. it was just another item. His dad had won the Academy Award when Frank Jr. was 10 years old. Back then, neither had any idea what a spectacular success one had to be to be presented with this statue.

"Can I hold it?" Marty asked Frank Jr., fearing a scolding or slapping of his hand.

"Sure. It's been sitting there for a decade. The only one who even touches it is the house cleaner. Just don't drop it."

Marty hefted the 8 ½ pound statue. It felt cold and heavy as he held it as if it were his. It was his for the moment. He was holding in his hot little hands, a gold Academy Award—Frank Sinatra's Oscar. It was a moment Marty still remembers to this day.

After calming down from his mental and spiritual epiphany with the gold statue, Marty followed Frank into a guest room where John Kennedy stayed in 1960. The room was pristine and covered wall to wall with frames. Small white picture frames. Each contained the most curious of mementos.

The frames were perfectly mounted on an exactly straight line at eye-level for the spectator to appreciate each, in the same manner you might see at an art gallery. They had been hung by a professional and each frame seemed to be like a vault with its contents secured behind a thick leaded glass, its contents meant to be seen but not touched.

In fact, it was a gallery, but the art was not a creative sketch or poem by some insane dead person. The other curious thing about art was that each appeared to be crumpled and then smoothed the way any paper looks after being waded up—the wrinkles a permanent memorial of the destruction.

During his stay John Kennedy would write notes to himself with a pencil and pad. Then upon review, he would crumple them up and throw them to the ground. These most unique handwritten thoughts of the President of the United States were framed throughout the room.

At one point Joey Bishop stopped in to say hello, Frank Sr. wasn't there so he didn't stay long.

Chapter Two—Las Vegas Nights 1965—1968

The Caesars Palace Band

By 1965, Steve Wynn had opened the Golden Nugget in the downtown Las Vegas area and the visionary hotelier sought to bring the biggest acts in to bring the crowds from the strip back to downtown Fremont Street. By this time, Marty had been on the road for three years and was looking to settle down and possibly tie the knot. The Caesar's Palace gig would make this all possible.

In a memorable encounter after rehearsal, Frank Sr. came by to greet the band members. Marty had met Frank Sinatra Sr. for the first time when the Tommy Dorsey Orchestra made several stands at the Sands, Frontier and Tropicana in Las Vegas in 1965. By the time Marty joined the Caesars Palace Band, Frank Sr. knew Marty fairly well as Frank Jrs. best buddy, and a top bass trombone player.

Marty always had a glass of water nearby to keep the horn and his lips well oiled.

"Marty," Frank said, "I hope that isn't water in that glass. You know what fish do in water?" This would be the start of a hot three-year stint that mixed Caesar's on the Strip with appearances at the downtown hotels, the Golden Nugget, the Fremont hotel and the Lucky Lady gambling houses.

Wynn had locked in Sinatra by putting together the best of Caesar's house band and conductor Al Ramsey. Marty took the seat once again at bass trombone and became a Stallworth of the horn section. He would also take the entire crew over to the Golden Nugget and the Frontier downtown to spread them around.

Nightly performances would draw standing-room only crowds and even though the headliner would be Frank, there would be no telling who else of the beloved crew might grace the stage alongside Frank. On any evening, Dean, Sammy, Peter, Joey, and any one of the number A-list entertainers might make a surprise appearance.

Rehearsals were the key to the live performances. This is where Frank would perfect his presentations. Even though the evenings were perceived as raucous nights of booze induced fun and games, Frank was the ultimate showman and perfectionist.

Frank would always saunter into rehearsals dressed impeccably but casually. The finest quality shirts, starched and crisp white, unbuttoned at the collar. A look of gentlemanly abandon. Although there were times he wore his, "He who wins with the most toys wins!" jacket. It was an interesting departure but not entirely out of character.

Often the straw hat tilted at the slightest angle made his look and feel smooth as silk. He'd glide into the rehearsal hall greeting all the musicians with the utmost respect. A glass was always nearby, but was it water? He never seemed the slightest off-kilter in rehearsals. Frank was the ultimate professional.

Rehearsals were disciplined and focused on perfection. Frank Sinatra, although not a formally trained musician, was the "best in the business." His years on the road with Nelson Riddle perfecting his arrangements equipped him to know each and every note. Frank's musical talent was innate. He knew his music and arrangements like the back of his hand—and you could hear it to perfection, night after swinging night.

Music scores for the orchestras in these days were hand copied and transposed to each instrument by hand. That meant that oftentimes, mistakes might be made in the replication and transcription process from one instrument to the next. Frank had a house in Los Angeles filled with the entire scores of all his music. Anything needed, a search through his music archives could include the entire orchestra score in multiple arrangements.

This is where the likes of Nelson Riddle and Count Basie conductor Quincy Jones help set Frank above the rest. The bossa-nova rhythms and swinging horn phrases could send audiences into a tizzy. And they were all written down among stacks of paper living at this lonely house in LA.

At one rehearsal, while getting through a new arrangement of "The Best is Yet to Come" Marty, following the hand-written score blew a wrong note. Thinking no one was the wiser the band finished the song, but Marty knew the mistake wouldn't be missed by the Chairman.

At the end of the song, Frank held up his hand and without even raising his eyes said, "bar 65, bass trombone."

Marty replied as he quickly corrected the copier's error onto his sheet music, "Sorry Frank, it should have been an E flat, not an E natural."

"Thank you, Marty," Frank said, and they rolled right into the next song.

After rehearsals the band would disperse for their evening meals and a little rest and relaxation in preparation for the 8pm and 12 midnight showtimes. But Frank would leave no loose ends.

Frank viewed every performance not as a simple night-club act, but as a full-blown concert production. He would show up back after a quiet meal, rarely juiced up before a show. He would check every facet of the stage, props and microphone so each show would go without a hitch. Of course, with the cast of characters who might grace their stage on any night, at least it wouldn't be the band and sound system to go awry.

But things could only be under his tight control so much. As the Rat Pack shows became more and more popular, the "drop-ins" became more unpredictable, and Frank didn't like the drop-ins or even worse, hecklers.

On this evening, well into the set, an A-Lister decided to drop-in on Frank's show. Paul Anka had been a chart-topper and Vegas strip regular for more than a decade when the Rat Pack hit Vegas. Paul had made a big mark in the industry both as performer and songwriter, and Frank might even credit him with one of his biggest hits, My Way.

So, the band was not sure what to think when the diminutive Anka unexpectedly walked on the stage as Frank was between songs and engaging in a light exchange with the audience members. Knowing Frank's penchant for the orderly, the band kept the mood going, tentatively.

Paul decided a great toast and tribute was in order so a short speech and many thank you's later, he finished his drop-in and walked off the stage. Frank hadn't said a word as he allowed the singer to spend his five minutes in the Chairman's spotlight.

Without a word uttered until Anka cleared the stage, the conductor anticipating the nod from Frank, he calmly quipped, "I didn't realize he was so short!" The band and audience roared.

So far as heckler's go, there was always one guy or gal with a little too much sauce, especially in the late shows. One of Frank's stand-byes was to interrupt the show, and with a gasp of exasperation proclaim, "Look buddy, I don't go down to the gas station and tell you how to pump gas!"

Pirate Kids

In the basement of Caesar's Palace below the concert hall there was a staff lounge and game-room complete with card table, pool table, ping pong table, a couple of couches and a TV. There was a fridge which typically contained sodas, a pitcher of water, someone's leftover lunch, some ketchup and relish. An old percolator-style coffee maker for those late nights waiting for the next gig sat next to a stainless-steel sink and a faded white linoleum countertop.

Since it wasn't an area accessible to resort guests it wasn't as pristine as the rest of the property, but it was functional and purposeful, and it was the perfect place to rest or even nap before the next show. There were scratches on the walls from past moving of furniture and equipment, and the room was sometimes used as a storage location when large production props or racks of wardrobe extras needed to be stored.

Marty, always the one to show up early, was going down to the game room one evening to the sound of young voices yelling and screaming. Two kids around 8-10 years old, a boy and a girl, were standing on top of the pool table sword fighting with the pool cues. With no adult supervision, the two were in a mortal battle for the mountain top. The talcum powder block was broken, and footprints of white chalk spotted the deep green billiard table top as well as the clothes, faces and hair of the young buccaneers.

"Hey, you kids, get the hell outta here," Marty yelled at the children, who were basically half his age. They turned in shocked surprise, dropped the pool cues and scampered out of the game room, one of them shouting, "I'm telling my Daddy."

Marty thought nothing of the encounter. He was more concerned about the pool table. He checked the felt, and it was covered in white chalk footprints but really not the worst for wear. So, Marty opened a soda, turned on the TV and flopped down on the couch half contemplating whose spoiled kids he just ran out of the room, and if he might have been too harsh on the kids.

Then, not so unexpectedly, Marty heard a voice coming down the hall. "Is this the person who used the word 'hell' and yelled at you?" Marty turned to see a small thin handsome man standing there with the two pirate kids. It was Bobby Darin. Marty would be rehearsing with him at 2pm. What a way to start a run, Marty thought to himself.

"Yes," they proclaimed in unison, "he yelled at us and told us to get the hell out."

Marty scrambled, "Mr. Darin, I'm sorry, but did they tell you what they were doing when I came in?" Marty held his hand out to show Bobby the pool table and the chalk footprints atop.

Bobby Darin looked sternly at the two and waited. The two urchins squirmed and looked at their shoes. Just a slight snivel and cough to break the silence.

Marty put the pressure on with a stern but not too aggressive tone. These were just little kids getting a little crazy, "Tell him what you were doing when I came in."

Murmurs, whispers, mumbling....

"Dodd Mitchell Darin." Said Bobby using the little boy's full name.

Marty took this short awkward silence to break the intensity of the moment and introduced himself in a friendly tone.

"Mr. Darin," Marty broke in. "I'm so sorry to have to meet you under these circumstances, I'm Marty Harrell, your bass trombonist in the house band. I'm a huge fan."

Marty stuck out his hand, not quite knowing what to expect next. Would he be fired? Disciplined? Bobby Darin shook it respectfully. Then turned his gaze back on to the two trembling mounds of jelly that were the two kids.

"I'm waiting." Darin commanded the children.

Bobby took one look at the talcum powder and shoe prints sprayed over the billiard green and the scene began to take shape. The matching powder on their noses and clothing also betrayed their antics. The blue chalk circle on the little girl's forehead gave the final indication of the tools and method of the attack.

All at once, the small boy blurted out his confession, "we were playing on top of the green table." He sobbed, as if confessing to the Lindbergh kidnapping—the little girl wishing she were invisible.

"Well, I don't think you are supposed to be standing ON TOP of a billiard table.....Do you?" He glared at the two scared puppies. "Do You?"

"No sir." Both kids looked down to the dirty carpet, tears streaming down their innocent faces, looking for a glimmer of hope that no punishment was forthcoming.

With the truth laid upon the table as it were, Darin continued to let them lightly off the hook. "Now, I think it would be appropriate for you both to apologize to Mr. Harrell."

"I'm sorry Mr. Harrell," they sang in unison, hoping their angelic expressions would end the torture.

"Apologies accepted," Marty proclaimed and shook the hands of the children, then with Bobby.

Then the two kids huddled with Bobby and whispered something of grave concern. "You better ask Mr. Harrell your question."

"Can we still come here to play?"

"As long as you behave yourselves, you're welcome here anytime." The kids were thereby successfully rehabilitated from their high-risk tendencies. It was a banner moment, and another life lesson, for the young Marty Harrell.

The Exploding Bass Trombone

One of the funniest situations that occurred during Marty's time with Frank Sr. occurred at Caesar's Palace during a live show. The crowd was raucous, and Frank was in full swing. On "I've Got You, Under My Skin," Marty would stand up for his solo. Dressed in his standard issue band tuxedo, he loved the moment in the limelight, not just for the crowd, but Frank would waltz over and stick his microphone right into the bell of the bass trombone.

The sound guys knew to dial back the mic so the audience didn't get blown away by the dirty brass swing solo. But on this day, things didn't go as rehearsed. The horn that Marty was playing was recently refinished.

Frank finished the verse just before Marty's highlight solo and came over as was his usual MO and raised the mic to the bell of Marty's trombone. For his part, Marty stood up and began his solo to the swing of the big band's rhythm section.

As Marty hit his first solo phrase, he felt a chunky clunk on the first valve. Then the bottom of the second valve exploded, and the internal assembly dropped to the floor, followed by a rain of springs, screw caps and small brass parts. The solo ended in a wheeze of off-key spittle. Marty looked at the ground in horror while Frank jumped back into the fray not missing a beat.

The band had never seen Frank split a gut laughing so hard, but they maintained the rhythm of the popular chart and the rest of the number went off without a hitch. Marty bent down and collected the little horn parts scattered on the floor and retreated to the music room during the next break to grab a new horn.

Nelson Riddle

By 1963, Nelson Riddle had been composing and arranging music for Frank Sr. for almost a decade. Along with his work with Nat King Cole, Dean Martin, Judy Garland and a host of others, he was riding a wave of success that included some of his own instrumental releases.

As a member of the famed Tommy Dorsey band and now newly signed on with the Caesar's house band, Marty and his bandmates all knew of, and worshiped Nelson Riddle. Frank Sr. had actually been on record owing much of his success to the "greatest arranger of our time." Of course, Marty's friendship with Frank Jr. would provide the opportunity for them to cross paths in the most informal of ways.

During a big coming out party held in honor of Frank Jr. and his burgeoning career, Marty found himself at the Los Angeles Ambassador Hotel and the Coconut Grove Nightclub, in his best black tuxedo, standing in a corner nursing a beer, while many guests and entertainers worked the crowd. Marty, who loved to hang back and people-watch, took in the festivities from a quiet corner of the club.

After a few moments watching the crowd mingle, Marty looked over to his left and noticed he was standing next to the legend himself, Nelson Riddle, who was also standing alone watching the crowd.

"I liked your playing tonight," Nelson commented.

Marty about fell over himself, "Well thank you very much Mr. Riddle, my name is Marty Harrell. "Marty wasn't going to miss his chance to get his full name out in front of the famed band leader. This is what dreams were made from.

"I know who you are, I got fired from your chair, you know." Marty knew that before becoming the world-renowned arranger, composer, band leader and even actor, he was a trombone player. But he didn't know he was a bass trombone player.

Marty was stuck like a mannequin, not knowing how to respond, but nodding his head and mumbling, "Really?"

"Yeah, Tommy (Dorsey) finally told me, 'you ain't cutting it at bass T' better try writing or arranging or something else." He chuckled at the foreshadowing statement.

* * *

They would continue to be friends but never worked together until another incident brought them together again, with Marty's daughter Stefanie.

In 1971 Nancy Sinatra opened at the International Hilton after a short hiatus from her debut in 1968. With this show she also featured her brother, Sugar Ray Robinson (the boxer turned tap-dancer), Hugh Lambert, and the Muppets!

For this show, Marty had daughter Stefanie for the weekend. At five years old he thought she was just old enough to hang backstage during the show. However, he wasn't quite sure that she'd be okay because he couldn't keep an eye on her during the performance and he wasn't quite sure if it was a good idea. On Frank's suggestion, "Why don't you take your daughter over to my VIP booth. She'll be safe there."

Sure enough, when they got to the booth there definitely was a couple there who he could trust with his 5-year-old. There in the VIP booth sat his old friend Nelson Riddle and wife—as well as Robert Wagner and Natalie Wood. By the end of the evening, it was "Uncle Nelson."

Jack E Leonard

Jack E Leonard was a popular comedian in the 60's with his Henny Youngman style satirical humor and witty one-liners. Often making his weight and bald head the subject of his self-deprecating humor. His dark suit, horn-rimmed glasses and bow tie were his signature look, and his sharp digs were the perfect warm-up for the band and their guests. Known as a pioneer of "insult humor" Jack became a regular on both television and Vegas live shows. Of course, Marty and the band knew him by the name Frank called him, "Fat Jack."

One of his favorite jokes was about the kidnapping of Frank Jr. He'd quip, "You know they heard him singing in the back seat…that's why they put him in the trunk!" Ba dum boom!

This circuit Jack E Leonard was the opener for Jack Jones. Later during the same tour, as Marty and Frank Jr. sat enjoying another early morning breakfast in the Flamingo Coffee Shop, Jack E Leonard and Jack Jones, who were playing the Flamingo that evening, were coming in for a bite. As the two Jacks walked past the table mumbling some one-liner about Marty's breakfast plate, Jack E reached down and grabbed the last sausage on Marty's plate, stuffed it in his mouth, and was gone to sit at his own table without missing a beat. He never even looked back.

Marty thought of a great come-back for the stunt. When the waitress came to check on them, Marty said, "See those two over there?" The waitress looked over and proclaimed, "You mean Jack Jones and Jack E Leonard?" Even though they might get to serve some celebrity on any given night, these two A-list entertainers weren't to be trifled with, if you wanted a nice tip. Besides, you never knew what kind of prank Jack E might have up his sleeve.

"Could you send over six orders of link sausages?" The heaping plate was delivered to the table a few minutes later. Once again, Jack E Leonard just started eating the sausages without even looking over at the boys. Marty thought he got him pretty good, and the boys shared a laugh.

To all their surprise, Jack E Leonard ate all the sausages except for one. This last sausage sat on the empty plate until Marty was once again engaged in conversation with Frank Jr. and preparing to pay his bill.

Jack E got up from the table and strode quickly toward the exit, sausage hidden in his hand. As he passed by the table, Jack E tossed the lone link onto Marty's plate and proclaimed, "here you cheap son of a bitch."

Substituting for the Count Basie band

Although a regular at Caesars and their traveling crew, there were no parallels to the '65 Count Basie orchestra led by Quincy Jones. The band could hit it hard and back the Rat Pack's standards and foolishness like no other. The tightest horn section in Vegas could wa-wa or run the mellow range of the trombone for charts like "Luck be a Lady" and "Fly me to the Moon." Marty at the time was working with the Caesar's House band but available to fill-in as necessary when the Count came to play with Tony Bennett.

Marty's schedule during Caesar's years would make your head spin. Marty would play Caesar's at 8pm and midnight with whichever headliners were in town, then between shows, he'd head over to the Frontier and play with Vic Damone at 10pm. In essence, playing bass trombone for another band during his well-deserved break between Caesar's band slots.

Bill Hughes was the bass trombone player for the Count Basie band when he needed Marty to cover for two weeks so he could take a vacation. On the first evening Marty was called to fill in with Count Basie, Marty arrived at the rehearsal hall an hour early to get the lay of the land and his hands on the sheet music. Everything seemed to be in place except for the bass trombone score. Marty asked for some of the stagehands, but no one seemed to know anything about the sheet music.

But as things went on in those days, the sheet music was nowhere to be found. The other musicians either had their own music or had the set down by memory, which was normal, but not helpful for Marty in his position. As show time crept closer Marty went to all the trombone players separately and asked if they had his part.

Of course, the bass trombone arrangement wasn't the same as the rest of the trombones, and since most knew Marty wouldn't be the permanent replacement, they all didn't even show up until it was too late to give him some hope.

Finally, about 10 minutes before show time, several of the horn players found the music and came into the showroom with the book in a box. It wasn't neatly organized in a three-ring binder. It was basically a stack of music pages, dog-eared, folded edges, covered with red and blue chicken-scratches.

If you've never looked at the music for an orchestra set-list, it could be hundreds of pages of sheet music, in a giant stack. Sometimes 6-8 inches tall. Not only were they not bound, but all the changes and mark-ups through the history of the arrangements were scratched on by the various musicians who sat in the chair previously.

"Here, sorry we couldn't get this to you earlier" the trumpet player said, not really too concerned about Marty's quandary. Chicken-scrawled and red-lined, the music wasn't something an amateur could typically pick up to back up the greatest singer of the era.

Marty sight-read the whole set—no one was the wiser—not even the Count!

The Fremont House Band

Around 1966, Marty was tired of life on the road, and many opportunities began presenting themselves all over the Vegas show area. Making the rounds through Downtown, Fremont Street and the Vegas Strip casinos, Marty took the spot at the Fremont House Band, next to the Golden Nugget.

Once again, a parade of the A-listers came through and engaged the crowds late-night along with Marty and his bass trombone. These artists included Barbra Streisand, Redd Foxx, Sammy Davis Jr., Steve and Eydie Gormé and a host of Vegas, Hollywood and New York elite.

Barbra Streisand was truly an A-lister and at the top of the charts when she came to Las Vegas with Redd Foxx. Marty, Redd and Barbara had originally met back in the late 60's in Tahoe and during the "kidnapping."

They all re-connected back in Las Vegas along with Benny Green, a trumpeter from the 40's. Barbra loved to play keno and begged Marty to join them. Marty had been around casinos long enough to temper his gambling, but keno seemed harmless enough. So, Barbra, Redd, Benny Green, and Marty all spent the afternoon and late into the evening playing keno.

Later that evening Barbra was feeling a little anxious and wanted something to help take the edge off. Barbra asked Marty if he knew where she could get some "grass," so Marty aimed to please.

It's fairly well documented that during this time, circa 1971, Barbra was alleged to have smoked marijuana joints with her band and even on stage during shows.

Later, as the show was coming to a close, Marty found a box with his name on it. It was a present from Barbra. A full set of her library of albums autographed with, "Stay high the rest of the year!"

Barbra was quoted as saying in an interview in Variety, "I tried it once and I didn't like the way it made me feel…" Little did anyone know that Marty might have been Barbra's weed connection in Las Vegas.

The Comedians

One of the greatest early life lessons Marty learned about the entertainment industry as a newbie was that they all looked out for each other. The industry could be brutal to those who didn't revel in the limelight. Many would spend their nights toiling away working the late shows, hoping for their big break, while spending the day driving cabs or waiting tables. It was understood however, once you make it, you help out others.

This was most memorable for the comedians. Marty worked with a whole slew of A-list comedy entertainers within the first couple years on the road and working Vegas. The likes of Jack Benny, Red Skelton, George Burns, Sid Caesar, Redd Buttons and Mickey Rooney all graced the stage in front of Marty and the band.

Redd Foxx had a series of tours in Las Vegas. In the mid-70's Marty would play bass trombone for Redd's Late Late XX show at 2am.

The comedians didn't necessarily need the back-up orchestra like the singers and dancers. Of course there was always the bumper music, the background, the introductions, walk-ons and the pun-busting, "ba dum bump." But they had an understanding and always requested the musical back-up, just to keep the orchestra working. If a comedian didn't ask specifically for the orchestra, the band would be out of work for the run. But it never happened.

The Mills Brothers

By the 60's, the Mills brothers had been in the limelight for over thirty years and were still going strong. Although by this time, the oldest brother was no longer touring with the group, their biggest hits included "Ain't Misbehavin'", "Jeepers Creepers" and "It Don't Mean a Thing." They were still a mainstay for the big band and swing jazz sound and could still pack them in each night.

Avid golfers, Marty would hang with the brothers at the Las Vegas Municipal Golf Course.

The three brothers would play into the rotation at many of the clubs Marty was playing at including the Fremont hotel downtown. The three were not only into their fourth decade of stardom, they were rocking the Vegas scene with not only their old standbys but also with more current charts like "Get a Job" and possibly their biggest chart of the 60's "Yellow Bird."

What most didn't know was that they were also huge baseball fans. During their shows, one of the brothers would ask Marty to keep a small transistor radio near with the earpiece in his ear. After each song, one of the brothers, whoever was closest, would lean over and ask, "what's the score?" Marty would use a series of hand signals to motion out the score. Sometimes he'd actually yell it out in order for the boys to hear it above the crowd noise.

This made for a very interesting gig as the brothers' mood could swing from hearty laughter and cheer to sadness and disappointment, in a matter of seconds, and the audience would have no understanding as to why.

Unicycle Juggler

The Fremont hotel showroom and venues at the time were still hosting many Vaudevillian style acts to open for the headliners. There could be a sword swallower, a guy who could play instruments with his nose, a woman who could spin plates on top of wooden dowels, knife throwers, hula hoopers, whistlers, joke tellers, magicians, contortionists, and of course, jugglers. Male jugglers, female jugglers, juggling teams, juggling kids, folks who juggled things on top of things and folks who juggled strange things.

Tonight, and for the next week, they had Betty Gorham, the unicycle juggler. A beautiful redhead in a blue stretch leotard. Juggling, balls, rings, swords, flaming batons, she could juggle anything. And she could ride any number of unicycles she had backstage.

She had the band playing the usual assortment of circus music as she started with the easy stuff and then got increasingly difficult and exotic. The fact that her royal blue leotard, with the orange fringe fit every curve and bump of her athletic frame was not lost on the gentlemen of the audience. It took very little effort to gawk at the spectacle rolling around the stage oohing, and ahhing to the extreme and increasing difficulty of each task.

First it was the colored balls—three, then four, then five. Then the fruit—apples, oranges and a cantaloupe. Then the dangerous stuff—knives and flaming batons. All atop the unicycle. First it was the short one, then the four-footer. By the time they got around to the most difficult part, the audience was looking up at Betty on a six-foot unicycle with bowling pins for the juggle. They were so heavy that she had to get up on the unicycle first from a ladder on stage, then an assistant had to toss the pins up to her one at a time, until she had them all.

For the grand finale, she would juggle the bowling pins while circling the stage on the giant unicycle—backwards! But that wasn't enough. In order to get the crowd going she would juggle the bowling pins while riding the unicycle closer, and closer to the edge of the stage—until it looked like she might fall into the audience. Of course, the people in the front row would catch a thrill from the near miss each time she came around.

The band was in on it too of course. Starting with the low escalating "Flight of the Valkyrie," to the drum roll, and crescendo at each near miss to the edge.

Then it happened. On the third night of the week, Betty was in full form coming to the grand finale. She was on the 6-footer with the bowling pins flying. While riding backward with the pins in flight, the wheel of the half-bike *just* ran up the bumper threshold of the stage, which caused her to check her momentum and look down, which caused her to slap the spinning pin with the back of her bespectacled hand and send the 3 pound, 6-ounce UFO careening into the audience.

There was an audible collective gasp as the whole audience watched, as if in slow motion, the bowling pin tumble, end over end, into the audience. An unlucky admirer, seated front and center, took the shot to the forehead and fell over like she had been shot.

The woman, wearing a black party dress and not-slightly inebriated, had been on the edge of her seat since the flaming batons and might have had a heart-attack anyway.

The audience screamed, the husband shouted, and Betty jumped off the unicycle and into the crowd like a mountain lion on the hunt in an unrehearsed stunt that was almost as impressive as the juggling itself.

The band ended the song with a blurt and folks rushed to the fallen woman who was later brought out in a stretcher. The gig was over for Betty

They had a comedian the next two nights.

The Merv Griffin Show and Jack Sheldon

Marty was at the top of his game by the mid-sixties. By the time he settled down to tie the knot in Las Vegas, Marty had already played with the most legendary artists of his time, including Sam Donahue, Quincy Jones, and of course, both of the Sinatra's.

Merv Griffin would often bring his hit television show to Las Vegas to film for a couple weeks each summer. Merv would bring the entire show, including orchestra, to Vegas for the stint, except that their bass trombone player was also a top studio musician in Hollywood and could never make the trip.

Marty would get the call and fill-in at bass trombone for some of the funniest, strangest and craziest spectacles of the Merv Griffin Show for five summers running.

Through this gig Marty met one of the funniest guys of the era. Jack Sheldon was already a world-famous bebop and jazz trumpeter, singer and actor. He then made television fame starring in the sitcom "Run, Buddy Run" about the adventures of an unlucky accountant on the run from the mob.

Jack was best known however from his trumpet solo on the Oscar winning song "Shadow of your Smile" from the 1965 film the Sandpiper.

Jack had such a quick and brilliant wit and became a favorite of Merv who would introduce Jack on every show, giving him an opportunity to crack the audience up with his dry wit and hilariously rude barbs that allowed Merv to have a giggle at the guests' expense.

On this taping, Jack took his opportunity to spread the recognition around to the rest of the players. He started at the top and began introducing the truly impressive musical talent behind Merv. Jack went on, "The All-Star band Ray Brown on bass, greatest bass player who ever lived. Jake Hannah on drums, Plaz Johnson on Sax, you know his saxophone from the Pink Panther. World Famous trombone player, Jimmy Cleveland, he's the only guy I know who has a summer home up his nose! And last but not least on the low down and dirty Bass Trombone, Marty Harrell." Jack didn't miss a beat.

Jimmy Cleveland was pissed, the band was laughing out loud on live television, and the episode would air on television in a week with most people not catching or making sense of the wry quip.

* * *

Big news broke on the set when it was announced that Tony Bennett was coming for an appearance. Because both Tony Bennett and Jack Sheldon had Oscar fame from the "Shadow of your Smile," it was decided that a special performance was opportune.

Rehearsal was scheduled the morning of the taping and Mr. Bennett was ready at 8am—bright-eyed and bushy tailed. Jack was late. They waited, then out of frustration started the "Shadow" without Jack. He'd just have to fill in. Rehearsal finished and Tony left, only slightly miffed. Jack was a professional and they had practiced and performed this number. The band director Mort Lindsey was livid.

It wasn't until rehearsal was over that Jack showed up. Undoubtedly because of his imbibement the previous night.

"Where the hell have you been? Tony was here at eight." Mort was at his wit's end. The band members just watched and waited for the upcoming ad lib."

"I couldn't find a parking space!" Was the outrageous reply. The band members just laughed and enjoyed themselves.

The Sword Juggler

Then there's the story about the Sword Juggler from Germany, the "Great Helmut." He was another of the Vaudevillian types, but his heavily Germanic speech made him an instant target for some friendly harassment and laughing behind his back.

His act consisted of juggling, of course, but this time with knives and swords. The knives would be in the air—three knives, then four knives, etc. His main variation was the balancing of swords on his nose—while juggling knives.

Although very dangerous and quite a spectacle, after witnessing Betty Gorman drop a bowling pin on a lady's noggin, the boys would always play in expectation of a foul. Of course, the witty Jack Sheldon would add his salt and pepper to the recipe for more laughter and spice.

"Please play Khachaturian's Sabre Dance once I am juggling," Helmut requested of the band. The wildly animated and nerve-wracking arrangement was perfect for the flying knives of the Great Helmut.

"Then when I balance the sword on my nose, please play a C major."

Jack came back with, "If you fall on the sword do you want a C minor?"

The band roared. Helmut just looked confused.

Liberace

Liberace was a regular at the Hilton during the late 60's. Of course, Lee—as many called him—and his persnickety nature made him a natural target for the pranksters of the band.

Liberace was of course known for his flamboyant cars that he would drive around on stage. The Rhinestone Roadster was actually a slightly miniature kit car fashioned to look like a Roll Royce covered in rhinestones which of course matched both his white rhinestone outfits and studded rhinestone piano.

The typical introduction would include some great band introduction, a glowing bumper speech beforehand, and then Liberace would drive onstage with the car, in his bespectacled suit, the piano awaiting him on stage.

So, it wasn't too much of a stretch for Marty to come up with the common childhood prank. The simple task of smuggling a potato onto the set was all that was necessary. While preparing for the show, Marty and Pat Houston snuck backstage and did the old "potato in the exhaust pipe" prank. It was Pat's idea, but Marty always brought a lunch box with him to rehearsal and Pat told him it was the best way to bring the "largest potato he could find" onto the stage. It would be too conspicuous in his front pocket Pat added to convince Marty.

Since Marty brought in the contraband, Pat was happy to take his part in the conspiracy. After rehearsal while everyone was breaking for lunch, Pat took the giant tuber from Marty's lunchbox and walked around the backstage area to check out the miniature convertible car. Marty took the role of lookout while Pat jammed the potato into the exhaust pipe. He actually had to kick it a couple of times to get it fully stuffed into the little tailpipe of the extravagant go cart.

It was typical on the set that as Liberace's opening approached, one of the stagehands would start the motor while the previous act was on leaving the stage so that the ignition wouldn't be picked up by the microphones. This allowed the car engine and potato to build up pressure just in time for the introduction.

As the intro bumper music was starting off stage where the band was, they could see Liberace in his white rhinestone matching outfit get into the convertible Rhinestone Roadster and noticed a gurgling rumble and cough coming from the car. It wasn't running smoothly but the time for the stage light was nigh.

The band played their assigned intro phrases, and the flamboyant pianist came in from the dressing room glittering like a disco ball. He jogged, but not ran, over to the little car. His hair was perfectly sprayed stiff, and he was as smooth as silk as he climbed into the miniature car ready for his big stage appearance and another Merv Griffin interview about his marriage prospects.

Liberace put the sputtering mini-Rolls into gear and started to drive it onto the stage. It coughed, sputtered and jostled him front and center like the car from the Beverly Hillbillies, and up to the piano where it gave a final sneeze, sputter and... BOOM!

The potato blew out of the pipe and hit the wall offstage with no evidence of its presence but the secondary crash. Liberace, and others, dived onto the stage like a mortar round went off! His hands wrapped around his head as he looked around to see what happened.

Everyone on stage ducked for cover and then, after taking inventory of their arms and legs, and seeing no one was injured by the assumed projectile, the audience chuckled and awaited the next surprise as if this episode had been planned. None the wiser about the potato gag.

* * *

It was well known that Liberace was quite protective and possessive about his pianos. He had his own piano movers, and no one was to touch them. During the Rhinestone Roadster appearances, the piano was a blaze of jewel and bling, only outshone by the owner.

Marty also played for the Merv Griffin show during their summer tapings. Sometimes on the Merv Griffin show a guest might get off script and there was no telling what might happen in front of a live audience. Today comedian and musician Pete Barbutti was a guest along with Liberace. He'd done his shtick and was on the couch with Merv enjoying Liberace's elegance as he masterfully tickled the ivories.

Pete was known for his outrageous hit-and-hit again comedy nuanced by his pageboy haircut and bulging eyes. He could play multiple instruments including accordion, trumpet and coincidentally, piano. His specialty was weaving his comedy bits in with musical punchlines and quickly belting out key musical phrases that ended with a verbal punchline, even ad-libbing song lyrics in response to a heckler or guest.

After Liberace finished his finale with a swirl and a bow, Pete unexpectedly, but not surprisingly, leapt off the couch and joined Liberace front and center leaving a dazed Merv on the couch speechless.

"Hey Lee (as Liberace was called often). You know I play piano too."

"Yes, I know that." Liberace eyed Pete then the audience in a cautious but inviting expression on his face.

"Let's play a duet together!" Before Liberace could protest convincingly, afraid to look like a prude in front of the audience, Liberace hesitantly joined Pete on the bench squeezing tightly together—Merv providing encouraging commentary—Liberace clearly out of his comfort zone.

Of course, Pete took the side of the bench closest to the audience to nudge Liberace out of the limelight on his own piano—an unthinkable act! Liberace, who hated to get off script, was too stunned to do anything but watch in horror as Pete started to play "Heart and Soul."

Starting with the melodic chords, Pete urged Liberace to play the one-key melody of the old standard, that almost every beginning pianist learns in their first year. When Liberace successfully took over the lower half of the melody, Pete started using his hands like a conductor and left Liberace to carry the tune awaiting the upcoming keyboard phrase of the chorus.

But when his moment came to pick up the melody Pete started playing the notes with his nose! Liberace was horrified but frozen like a deer in the headlights carrying on the musical spectacle until Pete finished and stood up sliding the bench away and taking a bow with Liberace!

Sammy's Party with Connie

Sammy Davis Junior may have been the most complete entertainer of the time. Not only could he sing—along with his pals—but his raw talent as a dancer, impersonator and comedian—made him the ideal short-man for the crew.

His tap dancing was legendary, an appealing rhythmic pitter-patter, but adding a little sand on the floor could render the "soft-shoe" to a melodic buzz. His vocal and dance interpretation of Mr. Bojangles, the homeless performer of the soft-shoe, would bring crowds from cheers to somber melancholy, to tears.

At the time very few appreciated the racial connotations of the entertainment industry. A quick look back at the Count Basie orchestra in film and there will be no doubt that the highest level of musicianship necessary for these great bands had no racial lines. Quincy Jones, the leader of Count Basie's Orchestra at the time, would back up Frank, Dean and the greatest singers and entertainers of the century.

Sammy's jokes however always could hit the common white crowds where they teased the most, but never to a degree beyond what would be acceptable for the period.

Connie Stevens was not just another Hollywood starlet making a splash on the Vegas circuit. By the mid '60's she had already made marks on television sitcoms, recording top singles, and starring on Broadway. Able to bring her singing and dancing talents to the Vegas showroom she was booked at the Flamingo for several weeks in the Summer of '68 just after her divorce from actor/singer/husband Eddie Fisher.

Fisher had magnificent success, scoring big hits for RCA Victor in his early years in the 50's and 60's. Although he had been on and off with his own Vegas show as well, those in the musician's circles thought that Eddie was really much better at acting than singing.

Recordings were one thing, if you made a mistake, they could dub over, and re-record over and over again—as many times as necessary. But playing with a live orchestra in front of a live audience was a different type of performance art—it was stagecraft, and Eddie was not as good at the dynamics of the live show and working with a conductor.

Yes, he could carry a tune, he had a solid vocal range and a natural vibrato, but his timing was horrendous. He didn't know how to follow the conductor. He would miss his cues, start early, then stop, and sometimes he'd get off rhythm and the band could never get him back on without a couple of circles around the chorus and bringing back the intro.

Marty had gotten to know Connie because between her shows at the Flamingo Hilton, she loved to visit the lounge at the Sahara down the street. After a couple of nights enjoying the lounge acts together Marty and Connie became a familiar item.

Tonight's act at the Sahara Lounge was a Vegas pioneer and favorite, unless you were part of his act. Don Rickles, king of insult humor, was going at the audience with gags and zingers that had the audience rolling.

Marty and Connie came into the lounge after he had already started and tried not to attract too much attention although that was kind of impossible since Connie was the headliner down the street and because of her sitcoms and charts, she had become a household name.

Marty, in his dark vest and white shirt, looked like he could be part of the show (which he was) or part of the hotel staff, but there was no way for Connie to walk around incognito. Her platinum blond hair and bright eyes drew the immediate attention of the comedic assassin.

Rickels couldn't pass up this opportunity to get some guffaws at Connie's expense.

"Hey ladies and gentlemen." He slowed his banter and shaded his eyes from the bright lounge lights as he made a spectacle of pointing her out to the whole audience, through the lights and smoky haze, trying to sneak into the lounge.

"Guess who just walked into the lounge, radiant and beautiful as ever?... She must be on her coffee break because she's actually starring in her own show down the street at the Flamingo Hilton! Ladies and gentlemen please give a rousing welcome to Connie Stevens!" Rickles announced.

The audience turned, oohed and ahhed, for several seconds straining to see Connie in the back of the lounge.

"Hey Connie, why'd you have to break up with Eddie? Couldn't you teach him to count to four? Ya know, 1...2...3...4?" He made the motions of a conductor waving his hands to the count. The lounge roared. Apparently, the little bit of musical trivia about her ex-husband wasn't exclusive to musical circles. Connie blushed.

* * *

Since Marty and Frank Jr., were regular hangers-out at the lounge they were often easy targets for the Rickles water-boarding torture technique, and who would be better to pick on than Frank's son, the kidnappee.

One evening, in preparation for the haranguing, the boys picked up a newspaper and took out the Funnies. They folded them under their arms as they walked into the lounge mid-Rickels. Once he spotted them, he started with the kidnapping caper and the bad singing jokes. In response the boys took out their funny papers and pretended to read them while sitting at a table front and center. Rickles was caught off-guard, and it took him all of about 2 seconds to catch up and rip them a new one,

"Come on guys, that's just a stunt, I know neither of you know how to read!"

* * *

It was from hanging out with Connie Stevens that Marty would first get to meet a musical legend that he would work with later in their collective careers, and these early co-mingling's would make for some interesting small talk about the "good ole' days."

It was after one of her Saturday shows that Connie invited Marty to join her at a party. The party was at the Sands Hotel Guest House being put on by Sammy Davis Jr. For their VIPs to feel more at home during their multi-week residencies, most casinos maintained a house nearby. The Sands Guest house was just off the East parking lot of the Sands at the very edge of the property. Just a short drive from the casino.

Marty picked up Connie in his Porsche 356 Roadster convertible—top down. Connie didn't have the most subdued do. In fact, once Marty started moving down the street, Connie's hairdo didn't and she screamed, "Stop this car and put the top up." Her hair was all over the place and Marty had no choice but to pull over and put the top up for the short ride across the parking lot as the hot desert wind with a light dusting of sand and mesquite was all that was needed to turn her big hair into a big mess.

The Sand's Guest House was unassuming and plain until they approached the door and started to see the Vegas-nightlife-looking people gathered around the door outside, music blaring inside. Once they got inside, it was dark, smokey and loud and Marty and Connie got separated when he went looking for a beer and she was pulled aside for some introductions.

Marty made a circuit around the house, then started looking around for Connie to ask her what she wanted to drink. Marty made his way into the kitchen where Sammy Davis Jr. was cooking a large pasta dish of his famous spaghetti and meatballs, and his secret garlic bread recipe.

Marty found a beer in the fridge and leaned against the counter to watch Sammy do his thing in the kitchen. As Sammy was stirring his tomato sauce and moving back and forth between the oven and the stove, he looked over at Marty and said, "If you've got your beer, you can go ahead and get out of the kitchen. I don't really like anyone looking over my shoulder when I'm cooking."

"Sure thing Sammy." Was all Marty could say. He turned around and made his way looking for a place to set himself down.

Having been kicked out of the kitchen by Sammy, Marty made his way to the large living room area where he could see a comfortable looking couch through the haze of cigarette and other types of smoke. He made his way to the couch but there was no place to sit because of the crush of people either sitting on the couch or standing in front of it. The only place to set his butt was on the arm of the couch.

Marty decided to do his usual, "lay low and people-watch" routine. He was sitting at the edge of the couch next to an attractive black woman with short hair but the heavy smoke, blaring psychedelic bass beat, and lack of lighting made it nearly impossible to communicate effectively.

He thought he should try to make some small talk mostly because it would be more awkward to sit there and say nothing, Marty wasn't an imbecile.

"How's it going?"

"Fine."

"Come to Vegas often?"

"Often enough." Came the reply, not offering much more. Silence...awkwardness.

"Nice party."

"Yeah." Pregnant pause…."it's a little loud." They were practically screaming at each other over the din of the music, crowd noise and clinking of bottles.

This went on for several minutes. Marty continued to scan the crowd for Connie and an obvious reason to get out of this spine-tingling conversation, but she wasn't around, and he really couldn't see through the haze anyway.

"So, I'm Marty, what's your name?" Marty shouted in the general direction of the woman but continued to gaze into the crowd.

"Dee….(something garbled)."

"What?"

"….onn….ick." Her answer once again buried under the muddle of the heavy bass beat and enthusiastic crowd noise. Marty made a face and turned directly at her for the first time to try to read her lips and associate it with the sound.

"I'm sorry, it's too loud. What's your name?" Just before she answered a third time, Marty recognized her face in a moment of shame. The music slowed and the din of the crowd settled for a few short seconds, and her annoyed response was heard by everyone nearby.

"Dionne….Dionne Warwick." She found herself shouting right in his face. Marty gushed in embarrassed agony. Dionne Warwick was one of the top charting female vocalists of all time second only to Aretha Franklin. Her decade-long partnership with Burt Bacharach and Hal David made her one of the top acts in Vegas in the Summer of '69.

It was an embarrassment that would quickly be forgiven by the easygoing Motown singer. She let him off easy as he fell over himself in apology and explanation.

"It's okay, I didn't recognize you either," she joked.

They would meet and work together almost 20 years later and share laughs about the time Marty couldn't figure out a way to get away from that awkward conversation.

"Oh, I remember you…" Dionne laughed heartily with Marty when he tried to explain their last encounter.

Satchmo's Gift Boxes

During Marty's Caesar's Palace years, many of his favorite stars and truly legendary musicians graced the stage right in front of the horn section. Marty never became bored or cynical with the trade. He was playing with the greatest entertainers of his lifetime, and he made the best out of every moment.

As a swing horn player, there was no one as big as Satchmo—the great Louis Armstrong. Going back four decades Louis Armstrong was not just a famous musician, he was practically the inventor, innovator and ambassador of jazz music. He was legendary not only from his jazz horn but also from his stage presence, scat singing and the gravelly-baritone voice that so many loved and identified him with. Marty was in awe playing behind his hero and legend in '65 when Louis toured Vegas.

Louis loved his band, especially the horns, and was known best as "Pops." On one elevator ride up from the band room. The shorter in stature king of jazz stepped into the elevator after Marty. As they both turned to face the doors, Marty noticed a little hanger-on on Louis' shoulder.

"Hey Pops," Marty didn't want to scare the seniorly gentleman. "There's a bug on your shoulder."

"Is he smiling?" Was the clever retort as he swiped the bug off his shoulder. Marty gave a healthy guffaw and they both enjoyed a light-hearted moment before stepping off the elevator.

At the end of the tour before the final show, Marty spied Louis directing a hotel bell clerk to offload some boxes near the band room. The boxes were stacked almost as tall as the trumpeter himself, and they didn't look like anything musical. Since Marty always liked to be prepared and showed up at the hall early, he was one of the first recipients of Satchmo's gift boxes.

Many of the stars of the time would have gifts for their backup orchestra at the end of their Vegas run. Frank had autographed photos of himself in front of the orchestra that read Frank Sinatra Orchestra Member 1965, and Barbara Streisand had little brass paperweights with a similar inscription. It was a customary way of showing appreciation, only the Satchmo version was from the heart, or maybe slightly lower in the body cavity.

"Here Marty, take one of these" he graveled as he hefted one of the fairly large and ungainly boxes onto Marty's grip. The box was about the size of a case of beer, but it clearly wasn't beer. It was a product that Louis swore by. Something he loved and felt everyone else should benefit from. Little did anyone know of the King of Jazz' love for regularity. Bowel movements were something he was not afraid to discuss, and regular bowel movements—he felt—everyone should have. And this particular laxative was his sworn favorite, the key to happiness and health.

He even became the unpaid spokesperson for "Swiss Kriss Herbal Laxative." Marty and the rest of the crew were each given a one-year supply of the healthy movement rendering concoction. A grateful, "Thank you so much Pops" was the standard response, along with an appreciative nod and smile, as each took several minutes to figure out what and why they had just been handed a large box of stool softener.

Burt and his Ponies

Later that year while playing with Caesar's band, Marty would work behind Dionne's partner in Gold Record crime, Burt Bacharach. After spending afternoons between rehearsals and shows hanging out, Marty would learn that Burt's expensive and exclusive hobby was Racehorses. He owned a ranch and bred and owned several of his own. Because of this expertise he knew the horses, the trainers, the jockeys, the breeders, the other owners. He knew the mudders, the rogues, the millers and the sprinters.

Between rehearsals and shows, they'd go to the off-track betting hall and Burt would tell them which horses to pick. He'd say, "pick Johnny's pride for the win. Then in the second race pick Country boy to show. Third race, go for Bickey Bug to show, and in the fourth race go with ShowMe Sally."

They'd clean up. For the time he was there, Marty made more money from horse racing than playing trombone. Marty recalled one of Burt's funniest proclamations, "Marty, I gotta get a hobby that doesn't eat."

The International Hotel

After Elvis Presley's successful '68 Comeback tour, he came to Las Vegas and the International hotel for several weeks of packed houses in the Summer of '68 and Elvis' big break-out year of 1969.

The post-Army Elvis had a new look in his black leather, tight-fitting suits and trademark locks. Now the screaming female fans were in their 20's and early 30's and just as wild about Elvis and ever. This would signal the emergence of the jumpsuit and the sweaty scarves.

Elvis had an uncanny ear for music. He wasn't formally trained, but his earlier experience singing gospel, playing acoustic guitar, then recording with a full band, then with the addition of his live electronic rock band, Elvis developed a breadth and depth in musical composition beyond compare.

It wasn't until Elvis came to the International Hotel, with the full orchestra, rock band, piano and backup gospel choir made up of the greatest female and male vocal quartets of the time, that the Elvis show truly defined musical extravaganza!

The new rock electric chords, mixed with jazz rhythms and gospel soul, backed up with bright, blaring horns, and soothing strings, would become a versatile music machine, borne of the traditional roots of American Swing, Chicago Jazz, and the Mississippi Blues. The message and image Elvis strived for was the antithesis of the drug-induced, long-hair, hippie people following the British Invasion and the Hard Rock phenomenon. His gospel songs with the obvious Southern religious overtones were sung from Elvis' patriotic heart.

With the full backing of a rock-band and a symphony orchestra, and gospel choir Elvis could wing-out the hardest, heart-pounding 50's rock beats like "Jailhouse Rock," as easily as a smooth samba or a classic swing of a Sinatra standard. The band could then woo the audience into a weeping blob with sad narratives like, "In the Ghetto" and then get them back on their feet to rock out to "Suspicious Minds."

The gospel sound overlaying the rock band backed by symphony orchestra was proving to be a live concert recipe for success.

Elvis wasn't a trained dancer either. In fact, if you were to compare the likes of Sammy Davis Jr., Gene Kelly, or any number of 50's and 60's entertainers, you'd find a depth and breadth of dance talent that ranged from ballroom, swing and tap. But through his early days and into the 70's, Elvis developed his own style of hip swiveling, pose-dancing, which would find their way into many other singers' repertoire over the next generation including Michael Jackson and the boy bands of the 90's.

Reliving some of the hip swinging, knee jerking moves from his early days, Elvis' dance move became a mixture of karate kicks and punches and poses and stances that threatened to tear the tight-fitting custom suits that became his trademark.

The final touch was the backing vocals. Elvis' gospel singing background compelled him to include a complete gospel choir as part of the band. Of course, these weren't just some raw recruits from a local glee club.

Elvis recruited the top talent of the day and many of those "recruits" would stay with Elvis through the remainder of his storied career.

The 1969 Vegas run was an 8:30 and Midnight show each night starting mid-summer and running through August.

The four-week schedule in the International was a huge hit—packed houses, twice each night. Following the '68 comeback they stumbled onto what was a new phenomenon to catapult the stardom of the King of Rock and Roll—the live "in concert" phonograph album. In August of 1969, the recording of the sold-out shows was memorialized in Elvis' first Live in-Concert Double Album.

With the release of "Elvis in Person at the International Hotel" in October of '69 and certified Gold in December of the same year, the new Elvis was about to take the country by storm. The decision was made to take Elvis on the road!

Chapter Three - On the Road with the King 1969 - 1977

The Elvis Presley Orchestra

In 1968, Bobby Morris was the music director and conductor of the International Hotel house band in '69 when the plans to launch a nationwide tour were being discussed. Elvis liked the sound they could bring together with a rock-and-roll band backed by a big-band horn section, backed by a gospel choir.

Then in '69, the Hilton company bought the International Hotel, and it became the famed off-strip Las Vegas Hilton—that would be Elvis' home through his career.

An exhaustive schedule was laid out that would take the band on a three-week city-to-city tour, then a week off back in Vegas. With dates and venues booked the logistics of organizing a full band would have to be worked out. It would be up to two players in the horn section to hire and prepare the bands for the tours.

The first year out, 1970, Joe Guercio and his key players, Marty and trumpet player Pat Houston developed the "Pick-Up Band" concept.

In the week before the next tour circuit, the three would travel to the home-base of the tour and hire contractors in the local area—3 trumpets and 3 trombones. Elvis' regular rock band ensemble traveled as a complete band, but the horns were picked up. And the arrangement and sheet music weren't necessarily all there either. In fact, what made Joe Guercio and the two horn players so good was that they could bring the band up to snuff with on-the-fly arrangements and, "let's play this, there" compositions. It made for an exhausting and unpredictable tour.

The other difficulty of bringing on the pick-up band in the first tours was that there was no sheet music. The rock band knew the songs and the horns just followed along. As they got further into the tour, they'd start to memorize their key phrases and lock down their ad libs. It wasn't until Joe decided that they needed to start doing things the right way that he put the right resources in place to make them real. That's when Joe brought on Don Hannah, a brilliant copyist/arranger who would stay on as Elvis' arranger until the end.

Once Don was on board, they started to get the scores written down and then followed with the musical arrangements for each instrument. And they got better and tighter each tour. The arrangements created a sound that could rock the house, swing it wide, and slow it down with strings like a nursery rhyme.

The set list could range from 16 to 20 of Elvis' most popular hits from the early days and include covers of the billboard top ten. Early songs like "All Shook Up" and "Hound Dog" were interspersed with popular 50's era hits like "Everybody Loves Somebody Sometime" made popular by Dean Martin and the Rat Pack types. New covers like "Sweet Caroline," "Suspicious Minds" and "In the Ghetto" would bring down the house.

But the sound that could be achieved with the versatility of the orchestra, rock band and vocal backers would make the Elvis Presley phenomenon something much more than a foursome rock and roll band like the British groups who'd come to the mainland.

The Elvis Presley Orchestra

The Rock & Roll Band

Lead Guitar	James Burton
Rhythm Guitar	John Wilkinson
Bass Guitar	Jerry Scheff
Drums	Ronnie Tutt
Piano	Glen D. Hardin
Electric Piano	David Briggs

Vocals

Harmony Vocals	Charlie Hodge
Backing Vocals	Sweet Inspirations JD Sumner and the Stamps Kathy Westmoreland
Other vocals	Sherril Nielsen

Orchestra

Conductor	Joe Guercio
Orchestra	Joe Guercio Orchestra

James Burton was previously lead guitar player for Rickie Nelson and had appeared on the Ozzie and Harriet show, he was also known as the Master of the Telecaster.

Jerry Schiff wasn't just a regular bass player. Most rhythm sections include bass, drums and guitar. Their job is to provide the timing and rhythm for the rest of the band and vocals. But Elvis' rhythm section was different. Jerry was a melodic bass player. Listening to any of the live performances, the rhythm section behind the King was anything but background. Jerry's fingers would fly across the fretless neck of his bass like a guitar solo in the lowest scales. Yet they provided the foundation for the rest of the musical and vocal talents to shine.

In later years Jerry would perform and record with some of the greatest rock and roll bands of all time including John Denver, Elvis Costello and the Nitty Gritty Dirt band. His most recognizable work may be on The Door's "Riders on the Storm."

Backing vocals included a gospel quartet of girls out of Motown. They would be a stalwart background for the entirety of the Elvis road tour. The upper scale was owned by the Sweet Inspirations. Founded by Cissy Houston (Yes, Whitney's mother), they included Myrna Smith, Estelle Brown and Sylvia Shumway. At the top of the scale was Operatic Soprano Kathy Westmoreland.

She was the white girl of the five. Sometimes if the Sweet Inspirations happened to stand on either side of Kathy, Elvis would quip in his low somewhat indiscernible banter, "You girls look like an Oreo cookie!" Go ahead, pretend you're Elvis and say it!

The lower scale was owned by JD Sumner and the Stamps. A gospel quartet out of Nashville and some of the lowest singers ever recorded. Along for melodic backing was Sherill Neilsen. These talents would bring a whole new sound and feel to his old rock-a-billy standards with their timed doo-wops, or bring the audience to a mournful trance during, "In the Ghetto."

Marty and the Greatest Idea of all Time

It wasn't until their fifth tour of that year (1970) that Marty may have had the greatest idea of his entire life, maybe affecting the lives of every live rock band performer since. Clearly Elvis was a true phenomenon. Women were crazy for him. The melancholy vocals, the swing of the hips, the rotating knees, now turned into outrageous jumpsuits with elaborate embroidery, rhinestones, sometimes a cape, and the signature dark sunglasses.

Women who may have been coming from their secretary job, prim and proper, were reduced to screaming throngs of middle-aged teeny boppers, who would do whatever required to get a touch, drop of sweat or a deep look into the eyes of the King.

The band members would love to ride the coattails of the king. Women were everywhere, but Elvis often traveled with girlfriend Linda Thompson for the recent whirlwind tour. But there was no reason the rest of the boys shouldn't take advantage.

As was typical for Elvis, he'd jump in a limo to the airport immediately after the gig, at which time the house announcer would declare, "Elvis has left the building." The women would instantly calm down, return to their pre-crazed demeanor, as if they'd been slapped silly, and slowly shuffle out of the building hoping to catch one more glimpse or scent of their "E."

Even though Marty had been living life on the road since he was 19, and had his share of groupies, settled down and started a family, he was now on the road again at least half of the month, and it was a grind. After Elvis was gone the band members always had a big band party on the second to the top floor of their hotel. Of course, the Colonel would book the whole top floor for Elvis.

Then the band and the vocalists would fly out together each morning on their own chartered turbojet airplane. Marty noticed that Elvis would bug out each night after the show, so the groupies would wait around then make their way home lonely again.

So, the greatest idea of all time was just a simple strategy. It was really just a simple request. It wouldn't cost anything, but it had to be done the right way. Marty presented the idea to the crew, and everyone knew it was brilliant.

Since Marty had been on the road with Elvis for a couple years, he was also tasked with making the request. The conversation leading to the execution of the greatest idea of all time went something like this.

"Hey Elvis, you know…since you just leave after the show, it would be helpful for us boys if you could somehow…you know, let the audience know where we're staying."

"Ahh…okay Marty…I get it! That's a great idea." Elvis smiled at Marty with keen understanding. So, each night at the end of the gig and just before signing off, Elvis added one more thank you to his list.

"And finally, I'd like to thank the (City Name here) Hilton Hotel for putting up the band members tonight." That was it! For Marty and the rest of the band it was the greatest idea of all time.

On the Road

The Elvis Presley Band on the road was a site to behold. An 18-wheel tractor-trailer was the key. This trailer would be the road home for everything required to put on a full-scale Elvis Presley extravaganza: bleachers, chairs, stands, drapes, and of course the most important equipment for the large venue, the public address (PA) system.

In these early days of live music performances, the Elvis Presley Orchestra, led by Joe Guercio, pioneered the use of the stage monitor system. Every venue or stadium always had its own in-house PA system to support whatever show might be in performance that night. What the band learned from the early days of the Las Vegas International Showroom was that the musicians couldn't really hear the music—at best, they were hearing the echo of their music bouncing off the walls or fading into the distance. What they could hear of the collective orchestra was an echo of the acoustic instruments being drowned out by the house PA system.

Musicians could not distinguish their own playing from the muddle. There was no way to ensure the musicians and vocalists could hear themselves. The stage monitor system was a separate sound system from the house PA. It was strictly for the band with on stage speakers (monitors) aimed back at the band members.

Each instrument was mic'd with its own individual microphone, and then their own audio was pumped back to them by section, or individual.

This allowed the sound guys to completely control the monitor audio volume back to the orchestra for each instrument. Elvis would have monitors facing him that would carry the full mixture of instruments, backing vocals and his own balanced voice in the mix. This method would be embraced as the way to manage the sound of every major musical performance since.

All instruments were mic'd, that is except for Elvis' acoustic. Even though most of his songs were performed with a full-bodied acoustic strapped-on over his jumpsuits, it wasn't plugged in or mic'd. This allowed him to play as much or as little as he wanted and no one could tell the difference.

And there were two semis. Both with the same equipment. So the rigs would leapfrog each other traveling from city to city while the other semi-serviced the show.

Then there was transportation. Roadies, equipment managers and laborers rode with the buses and sometimes with the band. Band members had their own plane, usually a chartered turboprop that could easily handle the eighteen band members, conductor, managers and support staff. Each musician was responsible for his own luggage and instrument.

Of course, Elvis had his own chartered jet and would fly himself, girlfriend Linda Thompson (when she came along), bodyguards Red and Sonny West, and Ed Parker.

The Colonel had his own private jet.

At the hotels, it was customary that Elvis and his entourage would occupy the top floor exclusively. In separate rooms on the top floor, Colonel Tom Parker and his crew, Elvis' bodyguards, Sonny Red West, and Ed

Parker (bodyguard and Karate instructor) and the tour manager and his staff. Any vacant room on the top floor stayed that way through the show dates.

The next floor down was reserved for the band (rock band, pianist, horns, strings, backup singers) and their crew. And there a party would be had following each show.

Not a Rock 'n Roll Band

Elvis was a gospel singer and very religious. Although not overtly religious in his shows, the inclusion of songs like, "How Great thou Art" and "Amazing Grace" allowed Elvis to share his gospel roots, and the audience loved it.

In the new era of Rock 'n Roll, Hard Rock bands like Led Zeppelin, the WHO, Rolling Stones, Black Sabbath and many more followed the bad boy trends of outrageous acts of performance violence, vandalism and destruction. Stories of trashing expensive musical equipment, knocking over speakers, and trashing hotel rooms were the absolute polar opposite of Elvis' image for the band.

He spoke of their professionalism and insisted that they be great guests at the hotels and venues where they stayed. It was typically the crazy women who brought the chaos and destruction with them as they climbed over any obstacle including other women to have the chance contact with Elvis.

Elvis didn't party like the crazy rock 'n roll bands either. Illicit drugs weren't being used out in the open. Elvis and the Memphis Mafia were popping pills and drinking excessively, but they were mostly a Bud, Jack Daniel's and cigarettes crowd. Needles and white powder weren't part of Elvis' party scene from what Marty had seen.

In actuality, Elvis loved to sing gospel at his parties. He would sing acapella gospel songs, and his friends would join in, harmonizing and taking turns late into the night.

Elvis actually had a gospel piano player that traveled with them just for Elvis to sing gospel music.

Of course there were always women present—always. But that's not the subject of this book.

The Opener

Many people are familiar with the opener for Elvis' live acts, starting with the musical score introduction from Stanley Kubrick's 2001: a Space Odyssey, but in reality the music comes from the 1896 performance of Also Sprach Zarathustra inspired by Frederick Nieztche's philosophical novel with the same name.

Why was this music melded into the rock classic CC rider used as the opener for Elvis' live show? The introduction, which became familiar in many households by the 1968 release of 2001, became the universally known theme opening fanfare for Elvis starting in the 1971 tour and through the end.

It was this "Sunrise" fanfare opening the best and most widely recognized orchestral fanfare for the biggest show on earth. Plus it didn't need any attribution or licensing. It wasn't the live shows that made this Elvis' trademark introduction so ubiquitous. It was the fact that it appeared on all his live albums that would seal the deal, and make it his own, worldwide.

In the final seconds before the show, the stage would be dark, and the stadium or house lights would go down. For several seconds the screaming, howling and crying audience would quiet down for a few pregnant, expectant seconds, then the noise level would rise again and fall as the band members would walk onto the dark stage.

The audience could see, feel, and sense the activity on stage. It was like watching Kabuki theatre preparing for the King of American Rock and

Roll. The anticipation would send electricity through the air and build as the maniacal fans sensed Elvis' presence backstage, standing right behind the curtains, preparing to show himself.

The Also Sprach Zarathrustra opening fanfare would start with the lowest horns, basses, guitars, pianos, as well, the bass and baritone vocals. Their harmonization would fill all the audible gaps in to create the rising crescendo as the timpani would add the in between, dum, dum, dum, dum….

As the fanfare would explode into the finishing high notes, the drums would roll in like a thunderstorm and the band would break into CC Rider and the whole stadium, house, or showroom would assimilate the rock and roll backbeat, Elvis would walk on stage, the scream and crying would rise above 100 decibels and another show would be making history.

The Sahara Tahoe House July 1971

The Conductor is more than just the start, stop and timing jock. The Conductor takes on many roles: behind the curtain, on stage and between shows as well. In fact, the between shows responsibilities could easily outweigh the on-stage responsibilities by leaps and bounds.

One of the roles that the conductor would take on alongside the band manager would be organizing and communicating to the rest of the band members. We're not just talking about the 4 horn players. We're talking about 4 trombone players, 4 trumpet players, the 5-piece Rock and Roll band (bass, lead guitar, rhythm guitar, drums and piano) but also at least 8 singers and an untold number of behind-the-scenes crew members, and sound men.

You can imagine this unruly group of artists, misfits and egos, all working closely together on a nightly basis. They were just like one BIG happy family, but they needed to be managed closely because of their rigid schedule and shared travel and lodging arrangements—they had to be able to get along with each other.

One of the most difficult tasks was rounding up all the band members for their transport to a new city after finishing a circuit. They'd all need to be on a bus, together to ride to the airport and get on their chartered turboprop for the flight to the next stop. One missing soul singer or tardy trumpet player could send the whole group to the mad-house or rushing like mad to the airport or next stop. One late person, and one person to find them creates two late people.

To address the chronic tardiness, Marty instituted a dollar-per-minute late fee to anyone holding up the bus. Each night after the set, a departure time was set and the word passed around. The money would be used to fund the after-gig party at the end of each circuit.

This last detail was implemented so that everyone would be agreeable with the penalty. Typically, the kitty could total several hundred dollars if more than a few people were more than 10 minutes late.

If the kitty grew large, the after party did too. And it wasn't uncommon for the band to glom together not just drinks, but catering for the best food, and even sometimes a band that they would hire to play for their enjoyment.

The Elvis shows and entourage graced Stateline, Nevada and the Sahara Tahoe for a late-summer two-week stint. Nothing was more beautiful than the Sierra Summertime. It was such a great departure from the episode in the endless winter snowstorm more than a decade ago.

The show would sell-out at 8:30 and Midnight each night for two-weeks straight. Even though the after-party kitty wasn't that large—with everyone booked solid into the hotel for two-weeks straight—there weren't as many opportunities for late penalty revenues—Marty had the hot tip for the party venue.

Many of the top casinos of the time, certainly including the Sahara Tahoe, not only ran the casino, hotel, showroom, lounge, restaurant, gift shop, and related sub-businesses, but also had private facilities for some of their big rollers. So, it was common for the casino to have a guest-house private residence at their disposal. Marty found out from his hotel contact that the Sahara Tahoe had just sold their last property and upgraded their guesthouse to a brand-new multi-level A-frame on the forested Northern edge of town.

In preparation for the after-tour party, Marty had lined up the Sahara Shores Trio, the nightly lounge act that played outside the showroom when they were all playing inside the showroom. They were a bass and rhythm threesome that could make more noise, to a back beat, than most rock and roll bands of the time. And they were real musicians. Marty spoke with them to line up the gig. They stated they had played at the guest house numerous times and would be there and ready to play when the band arrived.

The last show was scheduled for 8pm of the final tour date and Marty got the Sahara Shores Trio to show up at the guest house at 9pm so they could be set up to play as soon as the band started arriving around 930pm.

The band waited until the announcer gave the final call, "Elvis has left the building" to pack up their instruments and make their way to the new Sahara Tahoe guest house for a final farewell brouhaha. Marty rushed there ahead of the others to make sure the catering and band were all set to go. The guest house was a spectacular wood cabin with giant glass windows facing out toward the lake. A small patch of grass led down to a wooden dock.

The loft upstairs was actually a giant flat that was big enough for the band, their equipment and the whole party. So, when Marty got upstairs the food was there, and so was the booze, but there was no Sahara Shores Trio.

Marty waited for the band to show up anxiously as the rest of the orchestra, band and vocalists found their way to the guest house and party. Everyone loved the new party house and began to celebrate the tour closing but where was the band? It was okay with the stereo blasting, but most were expecting a little more than a record music for the tour finale party. Marty started to get some friendly harassment from the partygoers, and he started to worry.

He picked up the phone and started calling around, first back to the Sahara then to other contact numbers he had. Finally, he got a call back and it was Tommy D, leader of the Sahara Shores Trio.

"Hey man, where're you guys at? We've been warmed up and playing for an hour or so. What's going on?" Tommy was clearly annoyed and probably slightly worried they wouldn't get paid for the gig.

Marty had to shout on the phone so he could be heard over the din of the house party, "where the hell are you guys, I've been here for half-an-hour."

"We're at the guest house."

"We're all here now!?!........Which guest house? You mean the NEW guest house, or the OLD guest house?"

It turned out the Sahara Shores Trio was playing in someone's private residence for the last hour, drinking their booze and snacking on their food warming up and waiting for the entire Elvis orchestra to show up. Luckily, no one came home or ever found out what might have happened in their home. The Trio did finally get to the NEW guest house in time to give the guests their best rhythm and blues. And they got paid!

Pedal E & the Lowest Notes Ever Recorded

It was around the same time that Elvis came to the Las Vegas Hilton (formerly International) for a residency, and Marty was getting the reputation as one of the top bass trombonists in Las Vegas if not the nation, that Marty started taking liberties showcasing some of his rare talents. The bass trombone, as a representative brass for the lower register of an orchestra, is able to produce some very low tones. One of the lowest notes played on the bass trombone is Pedal C, theoretically. The "pedal" designation comes from the low scale of the pipe organ pedals.

When played on a bass trombone, Pedal C sounds like the rumble of a diesel turbine deep within the bowels of a cruise liner, or a tugboat blowing a foghorn in the harbor, or the flatulence of a giant beast like an elephant, or possibly a hippo submerged in anus deep water.

It's the type of sound that vibrates your spine. You don't necessarily hear it start; you just hear the low rumble when you feel it. Although octaves below the musical bass clef, these low notes are still in tune and can add a new dimension and feel to any song—and they were perfect to accent the multi-style, multi-tonal, complexity of the Elvis sound.

JD Sumner of Elvis' Gospel choir was similarly talented and renowned for his ability to sing at this low register. And Elvis liked to highlight his talent on stage. It wasn't until the rehearsal for the '73 Aloha tour that Marty started experimenting with some of these low notes during the live shows, and the best opportunity to showcase it was with the new cover for Steamroller Blues.

As they ran through the first rehearsal of the new chart, the band started in with the classic 1—4—5 blues rhythm, and horns (1-4-5 refers to the standard blues chord progression, such as A, D, E). Elvis came in on the first verse with his low, melancholy minor, then on the measure between, James Burton on lead guitar would accent the off-verse-measure with a blues riff—playing opposite Burton's lead Marty hit his note, but three octaves lower—"bbbrrrrrtttt."

Elvis waved his hands and stopped the music. "What was that?" Marty answered with another low burst—"bbbrrrrrtttt."

Elvis loved it and it became a standard fill opposite the lead licks for the rest of their time on tour, and even had Marty blow the low notes on the studio version. And it wasn't just Steamroller Blues. Listening back to the Elvis live recordings the low, dirty bass trombone can be heard in many other songs during the live performances.

Between JD with his low vocal range, and Marty and his dirty bass trombone, Elvis would often highlight their respective talents in a back-and-forth competition in singing and playing the lowest notes in their repertoire. At the time of these early live recordings, Marty and JD's competition marked some of the lowest notes ever played live and recorded.

Videos of this amazing performance can be found by searching YouTube for Elvis concert Live. See the link in the Video References at the end of the book.

Elvis wasn't the only fan of Marty's dirty bass trombone. His trademark beast audible can also be heard on recordings with Vic Damone, and Sarah Vaughn, who told Marty, "Baby, you sure can fart good!"

It was this special talent that earned Marty the nickname "Waddles" by Frank Jr., which sticks still today.

"In a backstage meeting with the author and Frank Sinatra Jr., in February of 2016, just a month before his untimely passing, Frank Jr. famously greeted Marty and shook his hand heartily declaring, "How've you been Waddles!"

The Cincinnati Hilton(s) November 1971

With such a large entourage traveling together, there were always opportunities for the band members to get confused or have logistical issues. Since there really were as many as 7 sub-groups, it was common that these types of errors could be compounded. You had the rock and roll band, then the female vocalists, made up of 3 to 4 ladies including founder Cissy Houston, a male vocal quartet, JD Sumner and the Stamps when on tour. Then the horns, which consisted of another eight gentlemen, then of course the band manager(s), support staff, bodyguards, and girlfriend.

It was always the band manager and the conductor who worked together to keep this quirky group of the most talented musicians in the business organized. But if the smallest clerical error or missed detail could cause quite a stir.

In November of the '71 tour, the band was scheduled for shows throughout the Midwest and then South. This week would take the entourage through Minnesota, Ohio, Kentucky, then down into Texas, Alabama, and Utah, with a couple of one-night stops in Missouri and Philly.

The tour was so confusing just thinking about the logistics will make your head spin. After bouncing between Kentucky and Massachusetts for gigs at the Spectrum and Boston Gardens, the group was scheduled to land in Cincinnati. They arrived well past midnight and the band would need to get right to their rooms and sack out as they had been on the road already for six days straight without so much as a break to have a haircut or get some clothes laundered.

By this time the logistician had the routine semi-down-pat. Upon landing at the airport, among a throng of worshippers often, the band manager, or sometimes conductor, would be first off the bus, to ensure order among the artists amid the din of freakish animals attempting to catch a glimpse of the King in travel.

Today it was Marty organizing the bedlam. A large manila envelope would be handed to the manager, and it would be his job to hand each band member their hotel key before boarding the bus that would take them by police escort to their hotel. Back then airport security was only a passing concern and the maniacal throngs—mostly girls and young women—would be crushed against the fences and gates with their instamatic cameras.

Once safely aboard the bus, Marty did the final headcount and gave the bus driver the nod. Today their destination would be the Cincinnati Hilton.

At the hotel, the band members were to go directly to their rooms—no dilly dally—until they were all in their rooms ready for a solid night's rest and another Elvis extravaganza.

Marty would be the last of the band members off the bus to bring up the rear and make sure everyone was accounted for. He waited in the hotel lobby to help or answer any questions. Then it began. The lonely desk clerk didn't really seem to know what was going on with the arrival of the bus full of seemingly famous people being followed by a throng of women in cars at such a late time.

The clerk's phone began ringing, and ringing, and then some of the band members started coming back down to the lobby. Their keys didn't work in the doors. The band members, taking up the whole of the second to the top floor of the hotel, tired and angry looking to get a good night's rest, started banging on the doors wondering why they were locked from the inside—all of them.

Guests were in their rooms when they were all collectively awoken by the confusion and angry band members standing outside their rooms. It was the definition of bedlam. Tired and angry musicians mixed with tired and woke-up hotel guests, made for a very confused late-night desk clerk who had to call the hotel manager for help.

Marty was as confused as the desk clerk, and they had to get the angry mob in order and calm down before the walls might come down. Marty questioned the desk clerk angrily, who for some strange reason had no idea the Elvis Presley band was taking over his hotel.

"I can't believe that you didn't have the rooms cleared out for us. Didn't you get instructions from the tour group about the arrangements?" Marty was trying not to be too nasty to the lowly clerk.

The clerk had seen this type of confusion before, "You know," he paused politely, having figured out their conundrum, "there's three different Hilton's here in Cincinnati. Are you sure you're at the right one? Because I'm pretty darn sure you're not!"

Marty put the blame on the bus driver.

Live from Hawaii—1973

The Hotel Opener

In the Fall of '72, the Colonel decided the Elvis phenomenon needed to go to Hawaii. Not only was Elvis still beloved from his bubble-gum movie days, but they could use the new technology of live television broadcast via satellite as the next big opportunity to splash Elvis on every television in the US, and the World. The Elvis Aloha tour would be scheduled to be broadcast Live via Satellite as the 1973 Tour opener. As a precursor, Elvis wanted to have a familiarity with the Honolulu International Center Area, so three shows were scheduled for November of '72.

News of the homecoming of Elvis back to Hawaii hit the island state like a once-a-decade monsoon. The Hawaiian fans were the most loving and committed. They loved Elvis and they demonstrated their emotion to the whole band as soon as their planes hit the tarmac of Honolulu International Airport.

As they boarded their bus that would take them, under police escort, to the Hilton Hotel Honolulu, Marty—who was conducting for this mini-tour—had an idea for a great treat for these very special fans that loved them so.

As the bus pulled up to the valet entrance to the Hilton, Marty went to the front of the bus to organize the troops. The raucous fans had formed a mob around the bus waiting for the band members to offload. They knew that Elvis was not there yet, news had preceded them that Elvis' plane, the

Lisa Marie, would be landing later that day. This welcoming crowd was for the band.

What could be more apropos for this crowd than Elvis' now-familiar and world-renowned opener, the Also Sprach Zarathustra—better known as the opening fanfare of 2001: a Space Odyssey. But this very special impromptu performance would be like no other, because the band lined up at the side of the bus in their usual line-up, but with no instruments!

The vocal range of the Stamps up and through to Kathy Westmoreland, the very highest soprano, along with the band members representing their instruments vocally, performed a live a'cappella version of the spine-tingling opener.

Standing in front of the lined-up musicians, Marty took his place as conductor. Waving the downbeat, JD Sumner and the baritones, along with Marty and the percussion crew started with, "Bah….., Bah…., Bah…..., BAH……., Bah, bahhhhhhhh….…, Dum, Dum, Dum, Dum…..etc." They did the whole opener up through the vocalized drum solo and the beginning of CC Rider before they finished on a high hold and took a deep bow. The crowd loved it!

Happy Birthday Marty

That same tour, it became known to the band that Marty would be turning 30 while on the islands. As Marty checked into his room, second to the top floor of the Honolulu Hilton, there was a wonderful surprise awaiting the bass trombonist.

A large basket of fruit, champagne and a message from the King, "Happy Birthday Marty, stay an extra week in Hawaii!" signed, Elvis.

Opening Night Baton Rouge, LA

By the middle of the 1974 tour season, the Hilton decided that Joe Guercio was needed back at the Hilton showroom for all the other acts, and couldn't be away half of each month on the road with Elvis. It was decided that when Joe wasn't along Marty would conduct.

Marty's first road tour as conductor of 1974 would be a two-week swing first through the southern states including Texas and Louisiana, then up to Iowa, New York, Rhode Island, and the back to Wisconsin. The shows sold out within days. Marty had had his fill of big stadium events, going all the way back to playing in the '64 World Series. But this time it would be in front of 16,000 screaming fans, crying girls, bodyguards and stage jumpers and Marty was in charge.

Marty was getting ready for this first time conducting for Elvis when they were standing together backstage. They could hear the roar of the crowd in the stadium and the buzz of the electricity powering the lights. Elvis was wearing a custom-made white jumpsuit with embroidery up the collars and around his waist. Although it was a marked change from the black leather, Marty figured, he's gotta wear something.

Show time came and Marty and the band walked on to the massive stage under the blare of screaming and fits in the stands and took their places. The excitement was palpable as the crowd readied themselves to be enchanted by the King. Little did they know of the anxiety of the young conductor about to start the show for the biggest entertainer of all time.

The band always started with Elvis off-stage and the low rumble of timpani to start the theme from "2001—A Space Odyssey." The crowd swooned and quieted to take in the big opener.

First the spotlight is shown on the center stage just giving the audience a glimpse of the master of the music. As Also Sprach Zarathustra's opening notes come from the horn section, a second spotlight would illuminate the 8 horns.

The house lights went down, and the spotlight shone on Marty. The nascent conductor waited to let the excitement build, the band waited for the downbeat from Marty, the crowd waited for the blare of the horns, and the King waited in thoughtful expectation, knowing something that Marty didn't know.

After a few tense seconds that felt to the crowd like ten minutes, Marty prepared for the biggest moment of his life. He looked at Elvis off stage and got the nod, waved the wand and gave the waiting orchestra the downbeat, the entire horn section lifted their horns and…...nothing. Marty waited, flinched, gave another nod and the downbeat and…..nothing.

Marty looked over at Elvis off-stage, who obviously knew about the prank, and he was doubled-over, laughing in his sunglasses and his white sleek jumpsuit with the embroidered trim.

The third time, Marty gave them the stink eye and shouted just loud enough so the band could hear above the din of the crowd, which was starting to build out of kinetic expectation, "Play God dammit!" And finally, they did! It was a great prank on the rookie conductor, played by the King. The rest of the show went off without a hitch.

The tradition of the high-exposure prank held up a tradition to be outdone. On the second day of the Houston tour Marty would return the favor to Pat Houston. The perpetrator of the previous night's distraction. The responding prank would be well thought out and prepared. Having hung out with buddy Pat Houston now for the better part of a year, Marty was familiar with Pat's aversion to things from the sea. Fish, shrimp, and particularly oysters were not on his list of preferred dinner selection. However, for some reason crab did not have the same negative effect on Pat as the other fishy fare.

Being that Houston was on the Gulf of Mexico and oysters on the half-shell were a particular specialty at every seafood bar, grill, restaurant and hole-in-the-wall, it was not a difficult task to find the right bi-valve to return the favor of the previous show. A short trip to the nearby market would afford Marty a small jar of fresh oysters.

Since Marty was conducting, he was there early checking all the equipment, and he just so happened to discover that Pat's trumpet was on its stand exactly where it should be minutes before a show in front of a crowd of 16,000 people. He kept his little jewel from the ocean in a little white Styrofoam cup. He had chosen the slimiest little oyster shot he could find.

Once again, they all lined up backstage in preparation for the day two opener. Marty made some snide comments about following the Conductor's lead. The group got the signal and marched orderly onto the stage and took their places. Elvis showed up in a Blue Leather suit with Indian jewelry adorning the fringes.

As the time came, Marty took his place front and center, he could see Elvis backstage ready for the intro, a couple of 1,...2,...3,.... and Marty looked over to the trumpet section to see Pat Houston in a fit, about something in his horn. Something small, slimy and fishy smelling. Something not at all of his liking. And something Elvis got another kick out of. Luckily, since they hadn't started, they were able to make a quick distraction giving Pat time to clean the oyster remains from this prized brass and recover to start "2001."

Black Angel

Elvis was a bit of a prankster in his own right. He had a great sense of humor and a quick wit. The problem was at his level of stardom, very few people could get close to him, or really get a taste of this humor.

One of his more notable gags has become known as the Black Angel. Elvis was always progressive in his social settings. The talented performers he worked with, traveled with, and trusted were a racially diverse group. And with his personal experiences growing up in the segregated South, Elvis had strong feelings and was known to express them.

After a great midnight show in August, Elvis decides he needs to make a statement at the grand Hilton Showroom. The wall held three 3-dimensional Court of Louis XIV sculptures of God's Heavenly Angels carved into the wall. They were lavish in their classical design yet tasteful and elegant. Elvis decided the trio was not diverse enough and with the help of Sonny and Jerry, painted the center lady black. It was a stunt Elvis was proud of and would show off as his handiwork when he mentioned it onstage.

Memphis Stop 1974

It wasn't until March of 1974 that Elvis' show would book into Memphis to grace the stage in front of a truly hometown crowd. The Midsouth Coliseum, in Memphis had 12,300 seats and could easily pack in all of Elvis' long time friends and family. It would be a proud homecoming for Elvis Presley. He also had big plans for throwing a party at his world-famous Graceland when the tour closed out in Memphis.

Marty recalls this show because it was one of the few times when he would be up close and personal with Elvis, especially if he was conducting. They'd been touring together for 4 years by this time and now that Marty was conducting at least half the time, he'd have much more interaction with Elvis and become much closer professionally.

Just before the show would start and during intermissions, as Elvis and the band prepared to go on stage, Elvis and Marty would squeeze over to the edge of the stage while Elvis would pull over the curtain just a skew, so he could peek out at the roaring crowd of screaming and crying fans. Elvis truly got a kick out of it.

On this great homecoming eve, Elvis' expectations ran high. Even though he always looked cool on stage, he'd be the first to admit when he was nervous. And it always seemed that when a show was being recorded for video and audio release, he would not hesitate to mention it to the crowd. It made him a real human being and caused much more screaming and crying.

Another item he liked to mention to the crowd was that his suits were too tight, and he was worried he might split his pants. That always brought a fit of hopeful excitement.

Tonight, it was moments before going in front of his hometown crowd. Even though many of his closer friends and family regularly traveled to his shows in Las Vegas and other big city tours of the past, this would be the first time many of his older childhood acquaintances and less affluent, distant relatives would ever have the chance to see one of his sold-out shows.

To ensure they got at least one opportunity, Elvis reserved the first three rows of the Midsouth Coliseum for his personally invited VIP list which included all those above and their lucky friends.

Elvis was peeking through the curtains in the first three rows. Marty was crammed up next to Elvis as the entire band got ready to walk on the stage in a friendly human crush. Elvis looked over at Marty and said, "I'm not exactly sure what's going on here." He had a sharp eye on those first three rows that he had dropped top dollar for.

"They're supposed to be reserved for my family and friends. I don't recognize anyone."

* * *

After the gig, Elvis invited the whole band to Graceland for a party. He had arranged catering and a band to play and have a great tour ending at the mansion he so loved. The last show was an 8:30pm show so they would be able to start the tour after party well before midnight.

In anticipation of a great party with the King at his digs the excitement was palpable. Many of the artists, musicians, and vocalists had never been to Graceland and without this specific invitation and opportunity, from the owner of the mansion himself, this could be a once-in-a-lifetime event.

The band members loaded onto the bus after the usual after-show housekeeping and luggage transporting. They chattered expectantly amongst themselves for the 15-minute trip down I-240 to the storied mansion.

Although not that late, it was a dark night, and the bus driver wasn't that familiar with the gated entry. First, he drove right past the entry gate missing the hard right off of Elvis Presley Blvd. He then had to take a couple of turns through a residential neighborhood to get back to EP Blvd. Then coming back, he cut it left a little too early.

Through the dark windows the noisy din on the bus turned quiet when they felt a hard bump, followed by a sickening crunch and scratching, squealing sound as the bus driver undercut the turn and ran over the curb into the entry gate.

The famously decorative wrought-iron gates resembling the treble and bass clefs, adorned with music notes and a silhouette of Elvis, was practically invisible at night since the mansion was closed, the moon was a sliver and the gate entry lights were low. After barely negotiating the turn, the bus driver ran straight into the unopened gates, tearing one clean from its hinges. The bus came to a grating halt that made the passengers' skin crawl and warned of significant cosmetic damage to both the bus and the once beautiful and ornate Graceland entry gate which laid under the tires of the bus.

The passengers off-loaded, did a quick looky-loo at the small scene of destruction and made their way into the grand famous mansion as it was clear no one was hurt, and nothing could be done until morning. Elvis arrived and shook his head.

"Don't worry about it." He didn't want the bus driver to feel too guilty.

Everyone knew that repairs would be forthcoming, and the damage would be forgotten within a week. Although the bus driver may have gotten the boot.

Girls, Girls, Girls...

Elvis' road manager Al Strada had told Marty that he was going to stay the night with the orchestra instead of traveling after the show with Elvis. The following morning for the final headcount, Al didn't show. The rest of the band members were ready to go, late penalties paid, but there was one more straggler. Al didn't know about the check-in time and dollar-a-minute penalty that he would be accruing on the clock. Marty also worried because he was one of the more "senior" members of the entourage.

After several minutes and risking a late departure Marty summoned security and went to check Al's room. Maybe he had overslept—or worse, maybe he had a heart attack or some other development.

Security joined Marty for the room inspection. No one home. The room was vacant, no bags or clothes. No Sign of Al. Then they went to check Elvis' room just in case. Again, the room was empty, of course, Elvis had left last night. Then...a sound. A banging sound coming from outside. They were on the 19th floor of a 20-story building, and no window washing was scheduled.

Marty and the security guy opened the curtains, and outside the window, on the ledge 19 stories above the parking lot, a woman was hanging on for her life, banging on the window with her shoe. They called Engineering and got her safely into the room. Al Strada had traveled with Elvis after the show and neglected to tell Marty. No late penalty was assessed.

* * *

It was the big stadium shows that afforded the crazed women another way into Elvis' arms. Since the stadiums were so large, they would actually drive Elvis in his limo, through the entry ramps, which were basically tunnels under the stands where the football teams typically entered through. Marty and the band would enter this way first and assemble themselves behind the curtains.

This gave them the opportunity to hover directly over the tunnel entrance and try to get a glimpse of the King from overhead. Once the limo started coming through the tunnel a loud crash was heard coming from the tunnel entrance. Marty and the rest of the band turned to see that a girl had either fallen or jumped from the seats above the tunnel and landed spread eagle on the hood of the limo.

Unsure if it was for alcoholic reasons, or just the impact of the landing that caused the girl to post up on all fours atop the limo's long black hood and… vomit, repeatedly, covering the windshield and hood with the murky colored ooze.

Elvis was nonplussed and only somewhat entertained. He quickly exited the limo and jogged the rest of the way behind the curtains with the rest. He chuckled and laughed with Marty and the crew and could only shake his head in disgust. The girl was taken away with only her feelings and stomach injured.

Later that year back in New York, Elvis and the band were back for three shows at Madison Square Garden. The balcony levels closest to the stage overhung the stage just enough for some dim-witted animal to believe they could launch themselves through the air and onto the stage into Elvis' arms.

Many probably entertained the thought but of course, one tried. She jumped off the balcony rail and dove forward throwing all caution to the wind (indoors)—why not? It was Elvis.

She landed on the stage with a big kaboom, and everything, including Elvis, stopped. As she tried to rise, she fell again and clearly had broken her ankle. She cried out and Red and Sonny rushed out on stage to help the girl. Elvis also stopped and ran toward the maimed superfan. Her leg was broken, and the boys carried her off the stage and to the medical unit. The show continued after the bedlam settled.

But it wasn't always the crazy dames coming at E. Sometimes Elvis' karate demonstrations would rile the manly men in the crowd, garnering their ire. Elvis was already stealing their girl's full attention, all they needed to inspire them was a little alcohol and another threat to their manhood. But this is exactly the reason Red, Sonny and Martial Arts Pioneer, Ed Parker—father of American Kenpo Karate, was Elvis' karate instructor and bodyguard.

After one of Elvis' karate demonstrations onstage, a serious looking thug jumped onto the stage and started to show off some of his own moves and challenged Elvis to a fight. This went on for less than a few seconds when all three, Ed, Red and Sonny surrounded the inebriated karate master and assisted him from the stage. He might have gotten roughed up a bit but no charges were pressed.

Elvis' Easter Bunny

It was on April 21st, 1973, the band was on a Western states tour and stopped at the Veterans Memorial Coliseum, Phoenix, AZ. They had just started the tour that would take them through California, Oregon, Washington and back through Colorado before returning to Vegas. This would be a bus tour because most of the stops, including Anaheim, Fresno, Portland and Seattle were just not far enough from each other to book the whole tour on flights.

The weather in Phoenix in Springtime was heavenly, but not that dissimilar to Las Vegas where many of the band made their home most of the year. They disembarked the bus and checked into their hotel rooms. Once again, Elvis and his entourage reserved the entire top floor of the Hilton Garden Inn.

It was here in Phoenix that Marty decided they would start the tour with a little Easter miracle for his good friend and Elvis band conductor Joe Guercio. Marty knew that Joe had a "girlfriend" in Phoenix and was making big plans to wine and dine her that evening.

Marty and Pat Houston—Marty's long-time prank buddy—took a stroll across from the Hilton where a nice little outdoor mall presented itself for them to pass the time until their big Easter show at the Veterans Memorial Coliseum.

They were almost out of ideas for a gag when they strolled by a pet store with a large banner advertising a sale on "Easter Bunnies." Marty's creative imagination and want of opening day pranks got the best of him.

They went into the pet store and Marty bought an easter bunny on the stipulation that he could return it the next day—and they could keep the payment—Marty basically wanted to "rent" the bunny. To which the proprietor agreed.

Marty had decided that Conductor Joe Guercio, who would be sharing dinner plans with a certain young woman tonight before the Easter concert, would be the appropriate target for the tour opening prank.

That evening while Joe was at dinner with his target audience, Marty snuck into his room and left the bunny, along with some food and a bowl of water in Joe's hotel bathroom, which undoubtedly would be a nice surprise for his date when she went to "freshen up." Apparently, they were out until late at night. By the time Joe and friend returned to the hotel room, the little bunny had tipped over the bowl of water, which neatly mixed with the rabbit food pellets and several pellet-ridden bowel movements of said furball, rendering the hotel bathroom a muddy, stinky mess. With soft cuddly surprise within.

The girl got grossed out and left under indeterminate circumstances and Joe came looking for Marty. After a good dressing down by the conductor, Marty gathered up the bunny in the cage and brought it back to his room for the pending return. Using the hotel towels to clean up the muddy mess rendered the room at least habitable, but the towels needed to be trashed.

Unfortunately, after the 3pm show Easter Sunday, Marty was in a major crunch. They were preparing to fly out that evening to their next destination, Anaheim California, to play at the Convention Center, the pet store was closed and there was no place to stash a bunny in a cage and keep him fed and watered. Marty considered leaving him outside the store but in the sunlight and no shade the bunny could easily overheat and die. Those who knew of the foolishness of the previous day were now bent on giving Marty the business,

"What are you going to do with that cute little bunny, Marty? Leave him here to die?"

"Nice going animal abuser!"

"We're calling the ASPCA!"

"Maybe you should cook him and eat him!" Were some of the comments.

Marty was nonplussed—he had an idea. Marty took the bunny in a cage down to the lobby where the usual pack of curious schoolgirls and former teeny boppers looking for a sniff of the King spied Marty, instantly curious.

"Hello ladies." He began as the girls, who knew Marty was with the Elvis Presley Orchestra because of his cool band jacket and sunglasses, started to gather around.

"Elvis needs some help. Would any of you ladies like to help him?" Stupid question. Marty was mobbed by anxious volunteers pressing for front and center.

Marty continued, "Elvis got this cute little bunny as an Easter present, but he can't take him on the airplane. Could one of you wonderful ladies take care of Elvis' Easter bunny?"

Several ladies volunteered, so Marty selected the most qualified and attractive volunteer and gave her the bunny, cage, food and all. Problem solved.

Later, as Marty was boarding the bus to the airport, the responsible bunny adopter was back. She had put a ribbon on the bunny's head, decorated the cage with a large ribbon and a sign. She and her girlfriends had it loaded in the backseat of a convertible Cadillac and were driving around the bus for everyone to see. The sign proclaimed proudly "Elvis—I'm taking care of your Easter Bunny—Love Sara."

Snowstorm in Pittsburg

The Nor'easter in December of '76 was one for the record books. The tour took the band to the Spectrum in Philadelphia. A great indoor venue that kept 16,000 screaming fans, safe from the blowing wind and snow. Lucky for the band members, they were only responsible for their horns. All their bags, chairs, music stands, and the sound systems were all taken care of by the roadies and local laborers.

So even though the snow hampered everything for most of the locals, the band members didn't have it so bad. The roads were evenly plowed through much of the city but the cars unlucky enough to be parked on the street side overnight might not be found and dug out for a couple of weeks.

The tour bus had dropped them at the hotel early after a quick flight from Kentucky the night previous. With the afternoon hours to kill, stuck in the hotel because of the elements, Marty, Pat and Howard Strobel, another trumpet player, were looking to put together a card game and get a little juiced up for the 830pm show.

However, there was not enough liquid for an afternoon of five-card draw and Marty and Howard drew straws and were volunteered to brave the elements and get some snacks and alcoholic beverages before dealing the cards. Pat and the others would stay warm and dry in the hotel room awaiting their return—Howard was not happy.

On the way back from the store just up the street and around the corner from the Hilton, Howard decided to pull a little prank in the virgin snow covering a square of lawn below the hotel. As Marty emerged from the package store, Howard decided to write Pat a message in the new fallen snow by dragging his boots on the lawn and drawing letters 10 feet tall in almost two feet of fresh power, to Pat Houston, 25 stories above. The letters were so big and clearly discernible they could probably be seen from the moon.

"F* * * you Pat" in giant letters on the snow-covered grass-lawn outside hotel was the message back to Pat Houston for his luck in drawing the short straw.

After the gag's effects had worn off, and the windchill began to sink into their bones, the boys made their way back to the room to take up the card game.

Marty found an instamatic camera to memorialize the event out on the lawn. They thought it was the funniest thing since sliced bread because anyone looking out the window on that side of the hotel would see the offensive words bigger than life, literally.

Marty called up to the room to see if Elvis and the mafia looked outside to see the funny message. Little did Marty know that since Elvis and girlfriend Linda Thompson had broken up after the last tour, Elvis was not alone.

"Hey Red, it's Marty, is Elvis there?"

"Yes."

"Can I talk with him? Have you guys looked out the window?"

Red, the big burly, soft-spoken body guard for Elvis paused awkwardly on the phone before answering.

"He can't really talk right now, and I can't explain what's going on."

"Is everything okay? Is Elvis okay?"

"Yes, he's fine. He's rolling on the floor laughing his ass off, and I'm not sure what's going on." Long pause on the phone, "There was someone here that wasn't turning out to be very, ahhh…. cooperative….when Elvis said he wasn't feeling very good and that she should go, she got angry and went out on the balcony...then she screamed bloody murder, like she was being attacked. But no one else was out there. Then Elvis went out to see what her problem was, but she just screamed, slapped him and stormed out of the room….?!?!?"

Marty asked, "What was her name?"

Red answered, "hmmmm….Patty."

Then it was Marty's turn to bust a gut!

Chapter 4 - End of an Era

The Crab Car

The 1977 tour year was promising to be another whirlwind for the Elvis Presley band. The show was becoming a mainstay of American popular music as the counterculture antithesis of the anarchistic and drug-induced themes of the British Invasion and the emergence of Acid Rock, and bands like the Who, and Led Zeppelin.

The Elvis phenomenon continued through their first tour in February '77 through Florida and South Carolina. Their second tour was scheduled to take them for three weeks through Arizona, Oklahoma, Texas, then to Louisiana, and ending in Florida.

The hectic schedule of two weeks touring and two weeks in Vegas was taking a heavy toll on the great singer. Secretly, Marty and the band members began to witness a transformation in Elvis' physical appearance and coherence starting 2-3 years ago. It wasn't that he was getting fat, it was bloating from the stress and strain of constant touring, partying, keeping late hours, and likely other types of prescribed and non-prescribable medications.

By the 1977 touring season Elvis was becoming more bloated, and less coherent. The bodyguards and managers would watch him like mother hens during performances for fear that Elvis would literally fall over in a comatose trance. His downhill turn didn't seem to affect his ability to belt out the tunes, however, and the rest of the band and vocals always combined to bring the house down as always, but the band members became more and more concerned, and more attentive to the heavily medicated superstar.

With the breakup from girlfriend Linda Thompson late in '76, Elvis' course of self-destruction seemed imminent. But the Colonel kept the touring schedule tight, and a full list of stadiums and events were planned for April, May, June and August to fill out the 1977 tour schedule.

As Elvis' obvious health issues and difficulties escalated, the tour stop in Baton Rouge in late March would mark only the second time that Elvis would miss a concert for health reasons. Eight supercharged years on the road would end the March-April tour with four dates getting canceled. Elvis was exhausted and depressed.

Even though Marty and the band had toured through the South many times over the last 15 years of his career, they were always on a schedule that didn't allow for any vacation or downtime. Marty's 30th birthday in Honolulu was the last time Marty remembered taking time off from his own performance schedule between Elvis, Vic Damone and house band nights at the Las Vegas Hilton.

So, with the rest of the tour canceled and only a trip back to Vegas to look forward to, Marty and his posse decided that a tour of the Louisiana Swamps would be an appropriate afternoon distraction. It was late March, and the Spring weather was turning more humid and sticky, what better activity than to venture further out into the Louisiana swamplands?

For this excursion it would be Marty, Pat Houston and Lu Dell formerly of the Louie Prima orchestra. Lu Dell was recruited to the Elvis orchestra after achieving notoriety playing trumpet for Louie Prima and Keely Smith.

The boys rented a car and loaded up for a day in the swamps—even though they didn't really know what that meant. They took State Highway 1 dead South looking to find the legendary swamps that they had seen pictures of but never experienced first-hand as Midwestern plowboys. They passed through White Castle, then Napoleonville, and the further South they drove, the more French the little town names became. After passing Thibodeaux and Montegut, they crossed onto state highway 56 and more or less ended in a little Bayou town called Cocodrie, Louisiana on the Bay Cocodrie. They were literally surrounded by a river, bay or swamp as far as they could see.

The 56 turned into Little Caillou Road and then the boys turned off on Shrimp Street and right on Redfish Road and found themselves at a bar/marina/shack called Boudreaux's Marina. After 2 and ½ hours in the rental car Pat, Marty and Lu exited the car looking to relieve their bladders and possibly fill them back up with beer. Inside the bar/grill section of the built-out shack, there was only a bartender and waitress with zero lunch patrons.

The humidity hung in the air like a wet napkin over their heads and shoulders. All types of dust, grime and insect parts would stick to their skin and hair just walking through the thick air. Mosquitoes buzzed around their ears like flying yapping dogs that wanted to suck blood, immediately attracted to their sweat and grime.

Inside, the place was decorated in a classic Cajun swamp bar theme. Fishing nets hung around the ceiling, with big cork floats at every interval. Starfish, sea-shells, and dried coral, all covered with a layer of dust rounded out the ambiance.

The only occupants sat at the bar and looked over as the boys entered the grill. The bartender was Renauld and the waitress (his wife?) Adelle. They looked, dressed and smelled like a stereotypical swamp-rat couple out of the storybooks—but in a good way. Renauld was unshaven with once-white tank-top, dirty khaki pants held up on one side with one-half of a pair of suspenders—a cigarette stuck to his bottom lip bounced up and down as he said with a Cajun/French accent, "Well looky here Adelle. Got some city boys come to the swamps to visit! What's your pleasure gents?" Renauld wore a fancy navy blue beret—reversed—that betrayed his French roots, but it was bare-threaded and ragged around the edges.

Adelle seemed to follow a similar theme with a dirty pink crop top, hanging off one shoulder and a black mini skirt that should have been about 4 inches longer, lest the boys see something that they shouldn't see hanging below the ruffle. Adelle obviously ascribed it to the European practice of keeping the natural hair about her body and looked a little like a bear wearing a miniskirt.

The boys ordered beers and sat at a table getting a load off and wiping the sweat from their brows.

"Are there any swamp tours around here? We're looking for a little Louisiana Bayou adventure," Marty stated matter of factly.

"Yeah, we ain't never seen no snakes or crocodiles, 'cept in the zoo." Lu added.

"Ain't got no crocodiles in the freshwater swamps, boy. It's alligators we got!" Adelle corrected Lu.

"I have a flat bottom boat, I'll take you boys around," Renauld offered. "We'll see snakes, alligators, swamp rats, and snapping turtles and who knows what else!"

The boys agreed and loaded up in Renauld's little wood dinghy with a 50 hp outboard, a cemented bucket for an anchor, and ventured out into the swamp. It was everything they imagined, fireflies, snakes, big furry rodents of unusual size—larger than anything they had seen in the city, and shadowy people who seemed to be watching them from afar. Or maybe it was just a feeling they all shared. It was a full day, just what they were looking for. But Marty started looking at his watch after 2pm, worried about the 2 hour plus ride back to Baton Rouge and returning the rental car.

When they returned to Boudreaux's Marina, Adelle had made a barrel of boiled crab for the gang and was waiting by the table to enjoy their company while they enjoyed the crab treat. Unfortunately, Marty was sad to announce they didn't have time to stay and eat them.

"You can't stay to eat 'em?" Adelle questioned, "I just steamed a $10 barrel of crabs for y'all and you ain't skipping out on the bill."

"I'm so sorry we can't stay, but we'll be happy to pay for the crab boil." Marty offered. It was only fair.

"Well, take 'em with you, you can eat them on the way home." Adelle and Renauld were satisfied.

The boys agreed, thanked Renauld and Adelle for their hospitality, successful day at the swamp and another memory for the books. But the swamp tour wasn't the most memorable part of the Bayou Trip. On the way home, the boys couldn't resist tearing into the barrel-sized plastic bag filled with steamed crustaceans.

First, they laid out newspapers they got from the marina and spread them out on the seats and floor, trying their best to keep the shells and detritus from messing up the rental car. The newspapers lasted a few minutes, but without napkins or towels to clean up a little after each tasty crab treat, the boys quickly became a sticky, slimy mess of crab carcasses and strange smelling crab-gook (it's the only word Marty could think of to describe the pasty grey matter that comes from within the crab body). By the time they finished with the crabs, the newspapers were a bunched up soggy mess, filled with the shells and gook that is usually wrapped up and slid from the table directly into the wastebin.

There they were in the car, and there was no waste bin. The car was the waste bin. By the time they were getting back into Baton Rouge, the car—which looked identical to the way it left, on the outside—had been turned into an indescribable pile of putrid sea creature remains. The smell was immediately identifiable. Any good Cajun would immediately recognize the smell of the crab boil and suffer pains and pangs of hunger. The boys ditched the car at the edge of the lot and left the keys. There would be no explaining or excusing themselves from this one.

Unchained Melody

The wonder and popularity of the Elvis show was not only the raw talent and chart-toppers, but it was in the rapport Elvis had with his audience. No matter how famous and glitzy his outfit, Elvis always seemed personable and down-to-earth. He would often, during a show, stop a song, apologize for a mistake, start back up again, sing a song while holding a sheet with the words, and have discussions with band members or even the audience.

After seven years touring and playing in Vegas, the band had seen pretty much everything. But Elvis still had some surprises for the audience and the band. In Binghamton, New York, toward the end of the show, just before doing the closing number, Elvis broke from the set list and declared, "I just recorded this...." He then walked over to the piano, which was typically occupied by Glenn Hardin, who didn't sing.

"and Charlie, I'm gonna need your help showing me the right keys." So Charlie Hodges had to get Elvis settled and hold the microphone in place while he sang.

Marty was conducting and looked over puzzled and held the band up from going into the next song on the list—Can't Help Falling in Love, for the close.

Marty and the rest of the band watched expectantly thinking, "What's Elvis doing?" The band and the audience then sat in awe as Elvis pounded on the keyboard and wailed the most amazing rendition of Unchained Melody most had ever heard. The band members were even more impressed because the audience had really no idea that Elvis had never rehearsed this before with the band, and that Marty and the whole of the Elvis orchestra were flabbergasted and jaw-droppingly impressed with the performance.

Elvis would add Unchained Melody to the set list through the remaining tour dates.

Tour 6—August 1977

The Fall tour schedule beginning in August of 1977 would be the sixth tour the weary band would embark upon for the year. Shows would open in Portland, Maine, then round into upstate New York and Connecticut, then finish in the Appalachians of Kentucky, Tennessee and Virginia.

Marty would be taking over as conductor of the Hilton Horns as Joe Guercio was asked to stay at the Hilton for their house orchestra, and Marty was ready to make some changes. One of the changes Marty planned was to highlight the band members and horn section more during the shows. He would have them stand up and get some spotlight during their key arrangements, instead of staying in their seats in the shadows.

In the beginning of the year, the band members had started playing their own mini solos during band member introductions, and it was becoming a bigger part of each show. Marty loved to let the horn section shine with an amazing arrangement by Don Hannah that left Elvis and the audience in awe. These great intro pieces can be seen and heard in many videos and recordings of the 1977 tour season.

For the tour opener starting in Maine, Marty had big plans to announce some of the new changes. To celebrate, he made reservations at one of the biggest lobster restaurants in Portland, the Portland Lobster Company. It would be a great way to kick off the new Fall tour season and his tenure as conductor.

The band charter plane would be taking off from LA with the band members there, then would stop in Las Vegas to pick up Marty and the rest.

From there they'd be flying directly to Portland for a nice lobster dinner affair and then kick off the tour at the Merrill Auditorium. A quaint little arena that would make for a very intimate and up-close show for the folks of Maine who'd never been graced with the presence of the King.

After picking up the remainder of the band in Las Vegas, they were off on their way to the Lobster capital. An hour into the flight, just as the band was settling into the building excitement for the Fall tour, and the highly publicized lobster feast that awaited them, Marty was summoned by the attendant to the flight deck. Marty ducked into the cabin with the pilots and was given a vague message.

"We've been given instructions to return to Las Vegas," said the pilot without any emotion or trace of knowledge as to why.

"No way." Marty was decisive. "We'd have to cancel tomorrow's opener if we go back. Absolutely not. Can we set down somewhere nearby so I can make a phone call and we don't have to waste all that time?"

The pilot agreed and got clearance to set the plane down for an emergency stop in Pueblo, Colorado.

No one knew what was going on as the plane started descending way too early for Maine. Marty announced that the pilots were instructed to land and that he had to make an important phone call. That was all the information he had.

After landing in Pueblo, Marty had everyone stay on the plane because he decided that the only way to avoid canceling tomorrow's opener would be if he could get back on the plane and head directly there.

Marty was pissed and was going to get to the bottom of this. As he got off the plane, an attendant of the airport had instructions for Marty to call the Colonel in Memphis. In the private plane terminal, Marty found an office phone and made the call to Graceland and the Colonel's private line.

The Colonel picked up the phone on the first ring. Marty could feel the cloud of doom cast over himself as he prepared to hear what he most dreaded but figured out could be the only reason for the summons. His spine tingled in terror and expectation.

"Marty," came the former carnival barker's voice. "Elvis just passed away. Send everyone back home to Vegas and LA." Click! That was it. That was all the Colonel had to say. No explanation, no sorrow, no apology. That was the last Marty would ever talk to the Colonel. Marty's whole world just blew up, and all the Colonel had to say was "Send everyone home."

Marty put down the phone—stunned but not surprised. They had all been thinking, worried, concerned about Elvis' health for years. It really wasn't a surprise. But it was earth-shattering for the conductor who now had the difficult task of telling the rest of the band, many of whom had been with Elvis many years before Marty. The walk from the terminal back to the unwary band members waiting impatiently on the plane was the longest and most difficult time Marty can remember. Marty choked back the tears in an effort to portray the stoic leader—a lump in his throat felt like a dry coconut. It was truly not believable.

In order to create the image of order, Marty got back on the plane and said without betraying his personal agony, "Everyone off the plane. I have an announcement to make." Marty then turned around and led everyone down the gangway and waited at the bottom a few yards away so the band could gather around.

"Quiet everyone." Marty raised his arms and shouted to quiet and control the confused and concerned mob. Marty didn't know any better way to go about this terrible task than just to spit it out.

"I just spoke with the Colonel. Elvis passed away this afternoon." Panic, shock, fear, and cries of woe enveloped the band and others crowded around for the unexpected news. The Sweet Inspirations collapsed in utter grief. Too stunned to do anything, a mass of questions, cries and shouting caused Marty to shout again.

"We've been instructed to get back on the plane and we'll be returning to Las Vegas."

It was the worst time of anyone's memory—a grief that would grip the nation as news of the King's passing made headlines. Elvis is Dead—age 42.

The untimely passing of Elvis marked the end of the tour and the end to the show that brought so much raw talent together to amaze and astonish a country of millions of sincere fans spanning multiple generations. Marty would continue to play for the Vegas casinos well into the 80's and 90's.

After his time touring with Elvis, he went on to play behind the best acts coming through Las Vegas. Frank Sinatra would make yet another Vegas comeback and Marty was the Stalwart bass trombone for many shows.

In many ways Elvis' untimely passing changed the course of history. It undoubtedly affected the band members on many levels: occupationally, personally, but they were more than just a band. They were a tight-knit family of amazingly talented individuals—each would be left to carry on with their lives and careers—many of them hugely successful in their own right.

For Marty, it marked the end of the road. It was an unexpected but well-deserved respite from the constant touring, sleeping in ratty hotel rooms and carrying his own horn around. Now he could settle back into his Las Vegas home and continue to play with the best in the business. Marty remained best friends with Frank Sinatra Jr. until his passing in March 2016.

Martin Harrell's storied reputation in the bass trombone seat would ensure his invitations back to play for Frank Sinatra tributes in the 80's and again in the 90's.

Video References and Endnotes

Frank Sinatra Jr. and the Tommy Dorsey Orchestra – See Frank Jr. sing Night and Day featuring a bass trombone solo from Marty Harrell.
Link: <u>Frank Sinatra Jr. "Night And Day" on The Ed Sullivan Show</u>
YouTube Search "Frank Sinatra Jr. "Night And Day" on The Ed Sullivan Show"

Uploader: The Ed Sullivan Show	Time: 1:22

Pedal E - Hear Marty play the Pedal E on the bass trombone.
Link: https://www.youtube.com/watch?v=GSTdyTxs2SA
YouTube Search "Elvis Presley - Live in Rapid City, June 21st, 1977"

Uploader: Jesse Garon Kottier	Time: 10:40

Horn Section - Hear the Hilton Orchestra Horn Section Highlight and see Marty play.
Link: https://www.youtube.com/watch?v=tU6p_6sN9fM
YouTube Search "Elvis Presley Rapid City 21 de junio 1977"

Uploader: Jorge Forte	Time: 1:00:00

www.ingramcontent.com/pod-product-compliance
Lightning Source LLC
Chambersburg PA
CBHW020247010526
44107CB00002B/138